Christmas Gifts
That Won't Break

Children's Leader Guide
by Daphna Flegal

Abingdon Press
Nashville

Christmas Gifts
That Won't Break
Children's Leader Guide

This book is printed on elemental chlorine-free paper.
978-1-5018-4006-7

Daphna Flegal lives in Nashville, where she is a writer and editor of children's curriculum resources. She is a diaconal minister in West Michigan Conference of The United Methodist Church, where she served in local congregations as Director of Children's Ministries and Director of Christian Education. She presently serves as lead editor for children's resources at The United Methodist Publishing House. Her favorite job is being a grandmother.

17 18 19 20 21 22 23 24 25 26—10 9 8 7 6 5 4 3 2 1
MANUFACTURED IN THE UNITED STATES OF AMERICA

CONTENTS

Missions Baby Shower

Collect new baby items for your local shelter or food pantry. Talk with the children about the kinds of items they can bring in such as disposable diapers, clothing, socks, blankets, diaper wipes, baby washcloths, baby shampoo, and so forth.

Wrap a large box with baby gift wrap, leaving the top of the box open to drop donations inside. Cut a large heart out of pastel paper and tape it to the front of the box. Write "Baby Shower Gifts for Babies in Need" on the heart.

Make enough copies of the "Missions Baby Shower" note (page 5) to send home with each child during lessons one, two, and three.

Missions Celebration

Angel Cakes

Prepare

✓ Provide angel food cake mix, ingredients and supplies needed for preparing cake mix, cupcake papers and pan, oven, marshmallows, whipped topping, table knife, napkins, and hand-wipes.

✓ Make cupcakes, following the recipe on the box of angel food cake mix.

• Give each child a cupcake.

• Cut a thin sliver off the top of each cupcake and set it aside.

• Cut a marshmallow in half lengthwise.

• Center half a marshmallow on top of the cupcake to make an angel's body.

• Add a dollop of whipped topping for the angel's head.

• Create wings by cutting the top sliver of the cupcake in half and placing half on each side of the angel's body.

Getting Ready for Baby Relay

Prepare

✓ Provide a diaper bag for each team.

✓ Place the unopened gifts in a box.

✓ Place the box on one side of the room.

✓ Place an empty box on the side where the teams will line up.

• Divide the children into teams and have them line up on the opposite side of the room from the box of gifts.

• Give the first child in line a diaper bag. Have the child run down to the box and place one of the items in the diaper bag. The child then brings the diaper bag back.

• The child takes the gift out of the diaper bag and puts it in the empty box, saying:

> I am giving this child the gift of (item placed in the bag). Go and get your gift for the child.

• Then the child gives the diaper bag to the next child in line the game continues.

Blessing Cards

Prepare

✓ Provide cardstock and crayons.

• Give each child a piece of cardstock and crayons.

• Have the children make cards of blessing for the babies and parents that will be receiving the gifts. If the children sign the cards, have them sign them from the class, the church, or with their first names only.

Adapted from PowerXpress! The Gift of Jesus © 2001 Abingdon Press and PowerXpress! Journey to Bethlehem © 2004 Abingdon Press

Christmas Gifts That Won't Break: Children's Leader Guide

Missions Baby Shower

In celebration of the birth of Jesus,
please bring one of the following items
to donate to a baby in need.

- ❑ diapers
- ❑ diaper wipes
- ❑ baby washcloths
- ❑ baby shampoo
- ❑ onesies

Art: Megan Jeffery
art © 1997 Abingdon Press

1 The Gift of Hope

Objectives

The children will
- hear Matthew 1:18-21;
- discover that the gift of hope is more important than gifts of things like toys and clothing;
- learn that Advent is a special time in the church year when we get ready to celebrate Jesus' birth;
- experience ways to give and receive hope.

Bible Story

Matthew 1:18-21: An angel comes to Joseph in a dream to tell Joseph about Mary's baby.

Bible Verse

Matthew 1:21: She will give birth to a son, and you will call him Jesus, because he will save his people from their sins.

Focus for the Teacher

Joseph's Story

Joseph is the main character in today's Bible story. The story begins with Joseph learning that Mary was pregnant. At first, Joseph reacted like a man who had been betrayed. Mary and Joseph were betrothed. In biblical times the betrothal covenant was as binding as marriage. Mary's pregnancy was considered adultery and legally reason enough for Joseph to divorce her. But the Scriptures tell us Joseph was planning to quietly dismiss her. Joseph changed his mind, however, after a good night's sleep!

An angel came to Joseph in his dreams with a message from God: Joseph was to go ahead with the marriage.

The Bible Verse

The angel also told Joseph to name the baby Jesus. Jesus is the Greek form of the name Joshua, which means "Jehovah saves."

> She will give birth to a son, and you will call him Jesus, because he will save his people from their sins.
>
> – Matthew 1:21

In Matthew 1:22-23, the Scriptures say:

"Now all of this took place so what the Lord had spoken through the prophet would be fulfilled:

"Look! A virgin will become pregnant and give birth a son, and they will call him Emmanuel. (Emmanuel means 'God is with us.')"

The gift of hope is given to us through a baby who will be God with us.

Celebrating Advent

Advent is the four Sundays leading up to Christmas Day. It is a time when we get ready to celebrate the birth of Jesus. The word *advent* means coming. We are preparing for the coming of Jesus.

Each of the four weeks helps us remember a gift—the gift of hope, the gift of love, the gift of joy, and the gift of peace. Christmas Day gives us the gift of faith. In the midst of the commercialism of Christmas we can give our children these God-given gifts. Unlike the gifts that we wrap and put under our Christmas trees, these gifts won't break.

Explore Interest Groups

Be sure that adult leaders are waiting when the first child arrives. Greet and welcome each child. Get the child involved in an activity that interests him or her and introduces the theme for the day's activities.

Name Art (For Younger Children)

- **Say:** Our Bible story is about Joseph. An angel came to Joseph in a dream and told him that Mary would have a baby. The angel also told Joseph to name the baby Jesus. Names are special.

- Give each child a precut bell (page 14).

- Encourage the child to tell you his or her name. Use a thick marker to write the first letter of the child's name in a large bubble letter on the bell. Take up as much of the space as possible. Write the child's full first name under the letter.

- Let the child glue small pieces of Christmas wrapping paper inside the bubble letter.

- Give each child a chenille stem. Show the child how to thread a jingle bell onto the chenille stem.

- Help each child punch a hole in the handle of the bell, thread the chenille stem through the fold and twist the ends together. The jingle bell will dangle from the loop.

- **Say:** You have your own special name. Your parents gave you the name you have for a reason. It's a special part of who you are. No one is quite like you. Mary's baby would have many names during his lifetime. Today we will hear about some of those names. Our Bible verse says: "She will bear a son, and you are to name him Jesus, for he will save his people from their sins" (Matthew 1:21).

- Save the bells to use in the "Ring It Relay" activity. (See page 10.)

Name Art (For Older Children)

- **Say:** Our Bible story is about Joseph and an angel. The angel came to Joseph in a dream and told him that Mary would have a baby. The angel told Joseph to name the baby Jesus. Names are important.

- Give each child a bell (page 14). Have the child cut out the bell.

- Have each child use crayons to print or sign his or her name across the front of the bell.

- Encourage each child to outline the name over and over again, using different colors.

- Have each child punch a hole in the handle of the bell.

Prepare

✓ Photocopy the bell pattern (page 14) so that you have enough for each child.

✓ Cut out a bell for each child.

✓ Provide: scissors, thick permanent marker (leader use only), glue, tape, small pieces of Christmas wrapping paper, paper punch, chenille stems, and jingle bells (one for each child).

Prepare

✓ Photocopy the bell (page 14) so that you have enough for each child.

✓ Provide: crayons, safety scissors, paper punch, chenille stems, and jingle bells (one for each child).

- Show the child how to thread a jingle bell onto the chenille stem, thread the stem through the hole, and twist the ends of the stem together to form a loop. The jingle bell will dangle from the loop.

- **Ask:** Who gave you your name? Do you know why they gave you that name? Were you named for someone in your family?

- **Say:** Your parents gave you the name you have for a reason. It's a special part of who you are. Mary's baby would have many names during his lifetime. Today we'll hear some of those names. Our Bible verse says: "She will bear a son, and you are to name him Jesus, for he will save his people from their sins" (Matthew 1:21).

- Save the bells to use in the "Ring It Relay" activity. (See page 10.)

In Your Dreams (For All Ages)

- **Say:** Many artists have used dreams in their art. One artist who did that was named Salvador Dali. He was called a surrealist. Surrealistic art is unreal—the rules of nature do not apply. Cows may fly and a dancing girl may have the face of a cat.

  Dali called his paintings "hand-painted dream photographs." He sometimes mixed photographs into the paintings.

  In the Bible, God often communicated with people through dreams. Today's story is about a man named Joseph. Joseph was a carpenter. He was engaged to Mary. Joseph heard messages from God when an angel came to him in a dream.

- Invite the children to briefly tell about some of their dreams.

- Show the children some Dali paintings.

- **Say:** Let's make dream pictures showing what you imagine an angel might look like. Remember, angels are messengers from God.

- Give each child a piece of construction paper.

- Have each child choose from the magazine pictures you have provided.

- Let the children cut out parts of the pictures and glue them onto the construction paper. Encourage the children to use their imaginations. The cut-outs might become the head or wings of the angel. The rules of nature do not apply.

- Encourage the children to use crayons, markers, or paint along with the magazine pictures.

- **Say:** The angel told Joseph: "She will bear a son, and you are to name him Jesus, for he will save his people from their sins" (Matthew 1:21). Now add the name Jesus somewhere on your picture.

- Have the children work the name Jesus to their pictures. If necessary, help younger children write the name.

adapted from PowerXpress! Good News! © 2002 Abingdon Press.

Prepare

✓ Check your public library for books that have pictures of paintings by Salvador Dali.

✓ Select pictures from magazines and catalogs that are clear, uncluttered, and appropriate. Tear out the pictures.

✓ Provide: construction paper; colored markers, crayons, or washable paint; glue; and scissors.

Christmas Gifts That Won't Break: Children's Leader Guide

Name Game (For All Ages)

- Have the children sit in a circle on the floor.

- **Say:** Names tell us who we are. Names help us talk to one another. If none of you had a name, I might have to say, "Hey, you with the red shirt, stand up." And if everyone was named George, no one would know who I was talking about if I said, "George, here is a piece of candy." Let's play a game and have fun with our names.

- **Say:** I will say my name when I snap the fingers of my right hand. Then I will say the name of one of you when I snap the fingers of my left hand. Then when we get to the snapping again, the person I named must say his or her name as everyone snaps the fingers of their right hands, and name another person as we snap the fingers of our left hands.

- Begin a clapping rhythm:
  Pat knees with both hands twice.
  Clap hands together twice.
  Snap (or tap together) fingers of right hand twice.
  Snap (or tap together) fingers of left hand twice.

- Repeat until the children are in rhythm. Then start the name game. Play until everyone has been named.

- **Say:** Today we are learning about what name the angel told Joseph to give to Mary's baby.

- **Ask:** What was that name? (Jesus)

- Help the children look up Matthew 1:22-23 in a Bible. Read the verses out loud or select an older child to read.

- **Ask:** What is another name for Mary's baby? (Emmanuel) What does Emmanuel mean? (God with us)

- **Say:** Let's play the game one more time and use these two names for Mary's baby.

- Play the game again with the names Jesus and Emmanuel.

Juggle It (For All Ages)

- Have the children stand in a circle. If you have large numbers of children, make several circles.

- Show the children the ball or soft angel.

- Begin by asking one child in the group to say his or her name. Then toss the ball or angel to the child.

- The child with the ball or angel then asks another child in the circle to say his or her name and tosses that child the ball.

- Continue the tossing until everyone has had the ball or angel.

- Repeat the game, trying to go faster each time.

Prepare

✓ Provide: a small ball, or an angel ornament or doll that is soft and unbreakable.

Large Group

Bring all the children together to experience the Bible story. Ring jingle bells to alert the children to the large group time. Use the transition activity to move the children from the interest groups to the large group area.

Ring It Relay

- Have the children move to an open area of the room.

- Mix up the name bells and place them face down on the floor near the Christmas tree.

- Divide the children into teams. Have the teams line up at the opposite end from the Christmas tree.

- At your signal, the first player from each team runs to the name pile and searches through the name bells to find his or her name.

- Then the players ring the bell on their name bell and then turn to their teams and shout out their names.

- The teams respond by repeating their player's name as loudly as possible.

- Then the players place their name bells on the Christmas tree, run back to the team, tag the next children in line, and then sit down.

- Continue until all the children have had a turn.

- **Say:** Each of you has your own special name. Your parents gave you the name you have for a reason. It's a special part of who you are. Mary's baby would have many names during his lifetime. Today we will hear about some of those names. Our Bible verse says: "She will bear a son, and you are to name him Jesus, for he will save his people from their sins" (Matthew 1:21).

- Encourage the children to hum "Away in a Manger" as they sit down in the large group area.

Advent Acts

- Present the drama, "They Shall Call Him Emmanuel" (page 15) to the children.

- **Ask:** Wow! How would you feel if an angel spoke to you in your dreams? How do you think Joseph felt after he woke up?

- **Say:** Let's take a poll to see how you think Joseph was feeling. If you think Joseph was happy, give me a thumbs up sign. (Let the children respond.) You could be right. Joseph may have been happy to know that Mary was telling him the truth. If you think Joseph was afraid, cross your arms and shiver. (Let the children respond.) You may also be right. Joseph may have been afraid to be a father to the baby that he knew was God's Son. A baby that people would call Emmanuel—which means . . . ? (Encourage

Prepare

✓ Set up a Christmas tree in your large group area.

Prepare

✓ Recruit older children, youths, or adults to be the Bible storyteller, angel, and Joseph.

✓ Photocopy the script (page 15) for the actors.

✓ Provide a flashlight for the angel.

Optional

✓ Provide costumes for the three characters.

✓ Set up the large group stage area to be the inside of a carpenter's shop from biblical times. Set out a hammer and pieces of wood.

✓ Place a mat or blanket on the floor for Joseph's sleeping mat.

Christmas Gifts That Won't Break: Children's Leader Guide

the children to respond, "God is with us.") There's another word that describes how Joseph may have felt. Let's see if you can guess what it is.

Word Play

- **Say:** Everyone stay seated on the floor. I'm going to play some music. While the music is playing, I will throw four beach balls out to you. I want you to bounce the balls back and forth to each other the whole time the music plays. When the music stops, I want whoever is holding a ball to stand up.

- Start playing lively Christmas music (""Joy to the World," "Angels We Have Heard on High," "Hark the Herald Angels Sing," and so forth).

- Throw the four beach balls out to the children. Encourage them to keep the balls moving back and forth.

- Stop the music. Have the four children holding the balls stand up and then come to the front of the large group.

- **Say:** Look. Each of the balls has a letter. Please hold the balls so everyone can see the letters.

- **Ask:** What word do you think this spells?

- Help the children arrange themselves so that the letters spell the word *hope*.

- **Say:** Hope. The angel's message gave Joseph hope. Hope because he could be sure that Mary's baby was God's Son. Hope because God's Son would save his people from their sins. Hope is a Christmas gift that will not break.

Speak It, Move It, Think It

- **Say:** Repeat the Bible verse after me. "She will give birth to a son, and you will call him Jesus, because he will save his people from their sins" (Matthew 1:21).

- **Say:** Now, let's add some movements. For "She will give birth to a son," pretend to rock a baby. For "you will call him Jesus" make the American Sign Language sign for Jesus. Touch the middle finger of your right hand to the palm of your left hand. Then reverse. For "because he will save his people from their sins," cross your fists at the wrist as if they were tied together. Then move your wrists apart as if you were breaking free.

- Have the children repeat the Bible verse again and do the motions.

- **Say:** Think the Bible verse silently in your head and do the motions.

- Have the children do the motions without speaking the words.

- **Pray:** Thank you, God, for your Son, Jesus. Thank you for the gift of hope. Amen.

- Dismiss the children to their small groups.

Prepare

✓ Provide: a CD with lively Christmas music, a CD player, and four large beach balls.

✓ Write the letters in the word *HOPE* on separate index cards. Tape a card onto each ball.

✓ Or write a letter on each ball using permanent markers.

Small Groups

Divide the children into small groups. You may organize the groups around age-levels or around readers and nonreaders. Keep the groups small, with a maximum of ten children in each group. You may need to have more than one of each group.

Young Children

- Show the children the Advent wreath.

- **Say:** This is an Advent wreath. Let's count the purple candles. (4) Advent is the four Sundays leading up to Christmas Day, so there are four purple candles. Each candle helps us remember how many weeks there are until Christmas. Today is the first week of Advent, so there are four weeks until Christmas.

- Point to the white candle.

- **Say:** The white candle is for Christmas Day.

- Point to a purple candle.

- **Say:** We light the first candle on the Advent wreath to remember hope. Hope is the feeling you get when you are sure you will get something you want, or when you are sure things will be OK. When Joseph heard the angel's message, he felt hope. Jesus gives all of us hope. Hope is a Christmas gift that won't break.

- Light the first Advent candle. Let the candle burn for a few minutes and then blow it out.

- Encourage the children to make Advent wreaths to take home and use with their families.

- Give each child a fistful of green play dough. Save a marble-sized lump of dough for each child.

- Show the children how to roll the dough into a six-inch length and form a doughnut shape.

- Place the dough onto a small sturdy paper or plastic plate.

- Mark the spot for each candle with a dull pencil point.

- Let the children place the four purple candles around the wreath.

- Help each child place the marble-sized play dough piece in the center of the wreath and place the white candle in the dough.

- **Say:** You can take your Advent wreaths home with you today and use them with your families to help you get ready for Christmas.

- Explain to the children about the collection of new baby items. Give each child a baby shower note to take home.

- Close with prayer.

Prepare

- ✓ Set up an Advent wreath with four purple candles and one white candle.

- ✓ Provide matches. (For adult use only. Keep the matches out of the children's reach.)

- ✓ Provide: four purple birthday candles and one white birthday candle for each child.

- ✓ Provide: a dull pencil, small paper or plastic plates, and green play dough.

- ✓ Photocopy the "Missions Baby Shower" note (page 5) for each child.

Make an Advent Wreath for the Small Group

- ✓ Arrange greenery in a circle.

- ✓ Space four purple candles evenly around the circle.

- ✓ Place a white candle in the center of the circle.

Art: Megan Jeffery © 2000 Cokesbury

Elementary Children

- Show the children the Advent wreath.

- **Say:** This is an Advent wreath. The wreath is a circle. A circle has no beginning and no end. It just keeps going 'round and 'round. The circle wreath helps us remember that God's love never ends.

- Point to the candles in the wreath.

- **Say:** Advent is the four Sundays leading up to Christmas Day, so there are four purple candles. Each purple candle helps us remember how many weeks there are until Christmas. Today is the first week of Advent, so there are four weeks until Christmas.

- Point to the white candle.

- **Say:** The white candle is for Christmas Day.

- Point to a purple candle.

- **Say:** We light the first candle on the Advent wreath to remember hope. Hope is the feeling you get when you are sure you will get something you want, or when you are sure things will be OK. When Joseph heard the angel's message, he felt hope. Jesus gives all of us hope. Hope is a Christmas gift that won't break.

- Let the children create Advent wreaths to use with their families.

- Give each child a six-inch paper plate, green construction paper, a pencil, and safety scissors.

- Have the children trace the paper plate to make two circles on the green construction paper, and then have them cut the two circles out.

- Instruct the children to glue one green circle onto the paper plate.

- Show the children how to use the safety scissors to fringe the edge of the second green circle.

- Let the children glue the middle of the second circle on top of the first circle, leaving the fringed part free of glue.

- Give each child five plastic bottle caps and some play dough or clay. Have the children fill the bottle caps with the dough.

- Instruct the children to glue one bottle cap in the center of the circle. Then have the children glue four bottle caps around the circle, spaced evenly. The dough side should be facing up.

- Show the children how to curl the fringed edges around the circle.

- Give each child four purple candles and one white candle. Have the children stick the white candle in the center cap and the four purple candles in the caps around the circle. Send the Advent wreaths home.

- Explain to the children about the collection of new baby items. Give each child a baby shower note to take home.

- Close with prayer.

Lesson 1: The Gift of Hope

Prepare

✓ Set up an Advent wreath with four purple candles and one white candle.

✓ Provide: matches. (For adult use only. Keep the matches out of the children's reach.)

✓ Provide: four large purple birthday candles, and one large white birthday candle for each child.

✓ Provide: pencils, small paper plates, green construction paper, safety scissors, plastic bottle caps, glue, and play dough or clay.

✓ Photocopy the "Missions Baby Shower" note (page 5) for each child.

Make an Advent Wreath for the Small Group

✓ Arrange greenery in a circle.

✓ Space four purple candles evenly around the circle.

✓ Place a white candle in the center of the circle.

Art: Megan Jeffery © 2000 Cokesbury

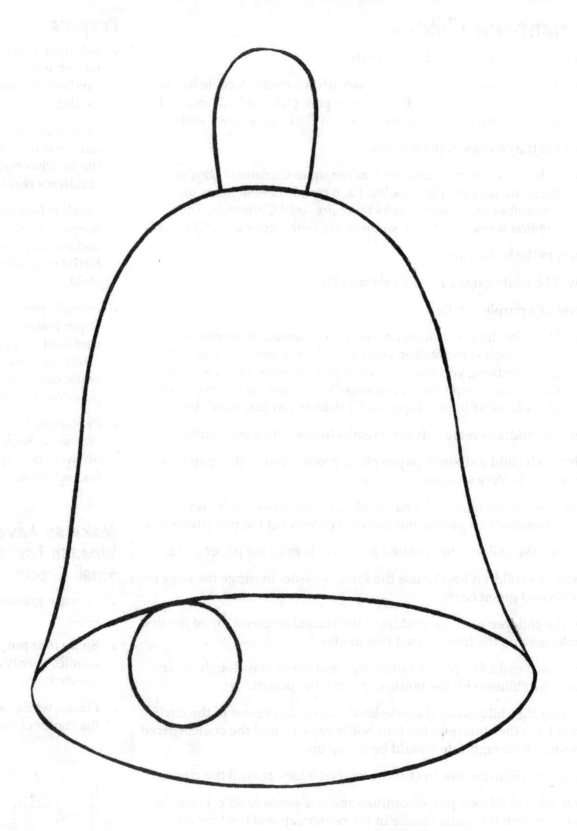

They Shall Call Him Emmanuel

by LeeDell Stickler

Bible Storyteller: Welcome to Advent Acts. In today's performance, we will present the story of Joseph, a carpenter in the village of Nazareth. He had been engaged to marry Mary, who also lived in Nazareth. But, as Act 1 begins, we quickly discover that something has happened.

Joseph: *(Holds up a hammer and piece of wood.)* I am a carpenter. I can make a table. I can make a bench. I can make a door. But today, I can't make up my mind. I need some help. Maybe if I sleep on it, a decision will come to me. *(Puts down the hammer and wood and lies down on his mat. After a few seconds, he starts snoring.)*

Angel: *(Enters, holding a flashlight to his or her chest so that it shines up toward his or her face.)* Joseph! Joseph!

Joseph: Hrumph. Go away. I'm sleeping. It's the middle of the night. *(Snores again.)*

Angel: Joseph! Joseph! You need to listen to me. *(Shines flashlight onto Joseph.)*

Joseph: *(Wakes up, startled.)* Who comes and wakes a man up in the middle of the night? This better be good. *(Sits up.)*

Angel: Joseph, something is troubling you. I've come to help. Do you want to talk about it? *(Shines flashlight around the room.)*

Joseph: Not really. But if I don't, you won't leave me alone, right?

Angel: Right! *(Shines the light back on Joseph.)*

Joseph: Mary is going to have a baby. She says the baby is God's Son. I don't know whether to believe her or not.

Angel: *(Puts flashlight to his or her chest so that it shines up toward his or her face.)* Pay close attention, Joseph. Mary is telling the truth, Joseph. Her baby IS God's Son. *(Shines the light back on Joseph.)*

Joseph: Whoa! *(Joseph puts up a hand to block the light.)* What do I do?

Angel: *(Puts flashlight to his or her chest so that it shines up toward his or her face.)* You give him a name—Jesus—because he is the one God promised to save the people from their sins.

Joseph: Jesus. That's a nice name.

Angel: *(Shines flashlight all around the room.)* He will be called by many names during his lifetime.

Joseph: Like what?

Angel: Some people will call him Emmanuel, which means … *(Puts flashlight to his or her chest so that it shines up toward his or her face.)* … "God is with us."

Joseph: So I should go ahead and marry her?

Angel: *(Shines light on Joseph.)* Yes, you should. This child will need you, just as the child needs his mother.

Joseph: That's what I'll do. I think I'll tell her … *(Starts to get up and then realizes it's the middle of the night.)* … first thing in the morning.

Angel: *(Puts flashlight to his or her chest so that it shines up toward his or her face.)* Good idea. *(Leaves.)*

Bible Storyteller: And that is just what Joseph did.

Adapted from Rock Solid: Middle Elementary, Bible Story Pak, Winter 2009–10, Vol. 2, No. 2, Session 3
© 2009 Cokesbury

Lesson 1: The Gift of Hope

2 The Gift of Love

Objectives

The children will
- hear Luke 2:1-7;
- discover that the real message of Christmas is God's great gift of love for each one of us;
- learn that Advent is a special time in the church year when we get ready to celebrate Jesus' birth;
- experience ways to give and receive love.

Bible Story

Luke 2:1-7: Mary and Joseph travel to Bethlehem, where Jesus is born.

Bible Verse

John 3:16: God so loved the world that he gave his only Son, so that everyone who believes in him won't perish but will have eternal life.

Focus for the Teacher

Bethlehem's Story

Luke reports that Augustus, who ruled Rome from 27 BC to AD 14, ordered a registration, or census, of the empire. Joseph was expected, as descendant of David, to register in Bethlehem, David's hometown. The trip was about eighty miles over often-rugged terrain. But even though the trip must have been hard for the pregnant Mary, it allowed the ancient prophecy to be fulfilled: "As for you, Bethlehem . . . one who is to be a ruler in Israel on my behalf will come out from you" (Micah 5:2).

The census also meant that lodging was impossible to find, so Mary and Joseph found shelter in a stable, probably a cave behind the inn. It was there that Mary laid her son in a manger.

Mary wrapped her baby in "bands of cloth." Known as "swaddling," wrapping the baby snugly in a long band of cloth was thought to make the baby feel secure and help the baby grow straight.

The Bible Verse

> God so loved the world that he gave his only Son, so that everyone who believes in him won't perish but will have eternal life.
>
> – John 3:16

John 3:16 is part of a conversation Jesus held with Nicodemus. Jesus explains to Nicodemus that the only requirement to a right relationship with God is belief.

From his humble birth on, Jesus was not the Messiah the people expected. Rather than a military ruler, Jesus was a teacher who tried to show the people how much God loved them and wanted to be in relationship with them. Jesus is a wonderful gift from God, a gift of love who came for all people of all times.

Celebrating Advent

This week you and your children will light the second purple candle on the Advent wreath. This candle helps us remember another unbreakable gift, the gift of love. The gift of love is given at Christmas, and all through the year, when we show our love for God, our love for our families, and our love for others.

Explore Interest Groups

Be sure that adult leaders are waiting when the first child arrives. Greet and welcome each child. Get the child involved in an activity that interests him or her and introduces the theme for the day's activities.

Preparation for Large Group Time

- Before the children arrive, make a large heart out of posterboard.
- Write the word *LOVE* in large letters across the heart.
- Cut the heart into five pieces.
- Hide the pieces around the room.

Prepare
✓ Provide: posterboard, scissors, and markers.

Welcome to Bethlehem (For All Ages)

- Invite the children to experience Bethlehem at the time of Jesus' birth.
- Set up several merchant booths. These may be as simple or elaborate as you wish. You can simply set out the supplies on a table, or decorate the room to be a biblical-times marketplace.
- Post signs for each of the merchants. Post additional signs that say things like "Welcome to Bethlehem, Home of King David," "Bethlehem, House of Bread," "Bethlehem Inn, No Vacancy," or "Bethlehem Inn, King David Slept Here—But You Won't!"

Prepare
✓ Make signs to post throughout your space.

Bake Bread

- **Say:** The name *Bethlehem* means house of bread. Bread was eaten every day in biblical times. Mary and Joseph probably packed bread to take with them on their journey to Bethlehem.
- Have the children wash their hands.
- Let the children work together to make honey bread. Have an adult bake the bread while the children are in large group time. Plan to eat the bread in small group time.
- Have the children mix together the following dry ingredients in a large mixing bowl: one cup wheat flour, one cup white flour, $1/2$ teaspoon salt, and $2 1/3$ cups nonfat dry milk. You may want to have the ingredients premeasured for younger children.
- Have the children mix together the following liquid ingredients in a small mixing bowl: one cup water, one tablespoon honey, and two tablespoons oil.
- Show the children how to gradually mix the liquid ingredients into the dry ingredients.
- Choose a child to oil and flour a flat pan.
- Turn the dough out into the pan.

Prepare
✓ Important: Be aware of food allergies the children may have before serving any recipe.
✓ Provide: wheat flour, white flour, salt, nonfat dry milk, water, honey, oil, a large mixing bowl, a small mixing bowl, mixing spoons, measuring cups and spoons, flat pan, oven or toaster oven, paper towels, and hand-washing supplies.

Lesson 2: The Gift of Love

- Have the children coat their fingers with flour.

- Let the children pat the dough until it is about a ¹/₂-inch thick.

- Prick the dough with a fork.

- Bake at 425 degrees for about 10 minutes or until it is golden brown.

- Have the children wash their hands.

The Carpenter's Shop

- Make sure you have plenty of adult supervision for this activity.

- Let the children enjoy hammering large nails into scraps of wood. If you have younger children, you may want to let them use wood glue rather than hammers and nails.

- **Say:** Joseph was a carpenter. He made things out of wood. Joseph was a carpenter in Nazareth, but there probably was also a carpenter in Bethlehem.

Prepare

✓ Provide: scraps of wood, hammers and nails with large heads or wood glue.

Swaddle the Baby

- **Say:** Mary would have brought bands of cloth to swaddle her newborn baby. She would have placed baby Jesus on a square of cloth. Then she would have folded the corners over her baby's sides and feet and wrapped bandages around the whole bundle to keep the baby's arms straight by his sides.

  People from biblical timess thought that a child's arms and legs would not grow straight and strong unless they were bound, so babies could not move freely for at least six months. The bandages were loosened several times a day and the skin was rubbed with olive oil and dusted with powdered myrtle leaves.

- Show the children how to swaddle a baby.

  1. Place the doll on the baby blanket with the head in one corner of the blanket.

  2. Fold the bottom corner of the blanket up and over the baby's body.

  3. Wrap one side corner and then the other side corner around the body of the baby. Tuck the corners of the blanket in place.

  4. Take one of the strips of swaddling cloth and wrap it around the baby from head to toe, being careful not to cover the face.

  5. Wrap the other strip of swaddling cloth securely around the baby several times.

  6. Tie the ends of the cloth in a knot, creating a loop. Slip the loop over your head, with the baby dangling on your chest.

- Let the children take turns swaddling the dolls.

- If you are using an old sheet or muslin, let the children tear or cut strips about three inches wide to make the bands.

Prepare

✓ Provide: cloth squares, baby blankets, or doll blankets; dolls; and strips of cloth or gauze, or an old sheet or length of muslin that can be cut or torn.

- When the last child has finished swaddling a doll, keep one doll swaddled. Plan to put the swaddled doll in the box manger during large group time (see the "Lullaby Relay" on page 19).

Salt the Baby

- **Say:** When baby Jesus was born, Mary would have rubbed his body with salt and olive oil. This custom was meant to firm and tighten the baby's skin.

- Pour a small amount of olive oil in the palm of each child's hand. Sprinkle salt over the olive oil.

- Have the children rub their hands together.

- **Ask:** How do the olive oil and salt feel? Does it make your skin feel tight?

- Instruct the children to wash their hands.

Prepare

✓ Provide: salt, olive oil, paper towels, and hand-washing supplies.

The Stable

- **Say:** Mary and Joseph tried to find room at the inn in Bethlehem, but because of the census, the inn was full. The innkeeper let Mary and Joseph stay in the stable. The Bible says Mary placed Jesus in a manger. The *manger* was a feeding trough—a box that held food or water for animals.

- Have the children work together to make a manger.

- Help the children center the smaller cardboard box inside the larger one. Be sure that the two boxes are the same height. Use strips of masking tape to hold the smaller box in position.

- Let the children crumple pieces of newspaper and stuff the pieces in the space between the two boxes. Let the paper come up over the top of the boxes.

- Have the children place crumpled pieces of newspaper in the bottom of the inside box to round out the box and give it dimension.

- Tear or cut brown rolled paper into long strips.

- Have the children crumple the strips.

- Show the children how to start wrapping the outside of the boxes with the crumpled brown paper. Tape the strips in place as you go.

- Let the children cover the inside of the smaller box with strips of brown paper.

- Continue until the entire box is wrapped in strips of paper and masking tape.

- Add straw if there are no children with allergies.

- Place the finished manger in your large group stage area.

Prepare

✓ Provide: two cardboard boxes that are the same shape and height but two different sizes.

✓ Provide: wide masking tape, newspaper, brown rolled paper, and scissors.

✓ Optional: provide straw.

Adapted from PowerXpress! In the Manger © 2005 Abingdon Press

Large Group

Bring all the children together to experience the Bible story. Ring jingle bells to alert the children to the large group time. Use the transition activity to move the children from the interest groups to the large group area.

Lullaby Relay

- Divide the children into teams.

- Have the teams move to one side of the room.

- Place a chair on the opposite side of the room for each team.

- Place a baby doll and a baby blanket or doll blanket in a basket or on the floor in front of each team.

- Show the children the swaddled doll from the "Swaddle the Baby" activity (page 18).

- **Say:** When baby Jesus was born, Mary would have wrapped her newborn son in bands of cloth. This was called swaddling. People in biblical times thought that swaddling a baby made the baby feel safe and helped the baby's arms and legs grow straight and strong. After Mary swaddled her baby, I wonder if she held Jesus close in her arms and sang him a lullaby.

- Hold the doll close to you, then place the doll in the manger from "The Stable" activity (page 19).

- **Ask:** What do you think? Did your mother sing you a lullaby when you were a baby?

- **Say:** Let's have a lullaby relay. Each team has a baby doll and a blanket. When I say go, the first person in line will wrap the baby in the blanket and then run with the baby to the chair on the opposite side of the room. Then he or she will hold the baby doll in his or her arms and sing the first four words in "Away In a Manger" to the doll. Finally he or she will run back to the team and give the doll to the next person, who will continue the relay. The first person will go to end of the line and sit down. If the doll becomes unwrapped, you must stop and rewrap the doll.

- Make sure everyone understands the relay and then say, "Go!"

- Continue the relay until every child has a turn.

- Encourage the children to hum "Away in a Manger" as they sit down in the large group area.

Advent Acts

- **Say:** We're going to add sound effects to today's Bible story. First we need to get into sound effect teams.

Prepare

✓ Provide for each team: a chair, a baby doll, and a baby blanket or doll blanket.

✓ Optional: provide baskets.

Prepare

✓ Photocopy "Jesus Is Born" (page 25) for your storyteller.

Christmas Gifts That Won't Break: Children's Leader Guide

- Divide the children into five sound effects teams.

- Explain the sound effects to each team.

> Team 1: trumpets—with fists to mouth, make a trumpet sound.
> Team 2: donkey hooves—with cupped hands, pat right and left knees alternately.
> Team 3: crowd—with cupped hands to mouth, repeat the phrase "peas and carrots" over and over again.
> Team 4: door sounds—knock on a chair or the floor.
> Team 5: animals of the stable—variety of animal sounds (cow, sheep, donkey, rooster, doves, and so forth).

- Present the drama, "Jesus Is Born" (page 25) to the children and encourage the children to provide the sound effects.

Word Play

- **Say:** Everyone stay seated on the floor in your teams. I want each team to choose a leader. Then I want everyone else on your team to line up behind the leader and put your hands on the person's shoulders in front of you. Somewhere in this room there are five puzzle pieces. I'm going to play some music. While the music is playing, I want each team to search for one puzzle piece. When your team finds a piece, the leader should pick up the piece and then sit down in our large group area. While you are searching, your team must stay connected.

- Play Christmas music and have the teams find the puzzle pieces.

- When all the puzzle pieces are found, have the teams sit down.

- Have the team leaders bring the puzzle pieces to the front.

- Tape the puzzle together.

- **Ask:** What does the puzzle say? *(love)* Tell me again, what does the puzzle say? *(Encourage the children to shout, love.)*

- **Say:** Love. God loved us so much that he sent his son, Jesus. God loves us and we can show our love for God by loving others. Love is a Christmas gift that will not break.

Bible Verse Echo

- Our Bible verse is about God's gift of love. It is a gift God gives to each one of us. As I say our Bible verse, repeat it after me, using the same tone, volume, and speed as I do.

- Using the "break points" below, have the children echo the Bible verse. Use loud/soft, and emphasize the bold words. Repeat the verse several times using a variety of styles.

- **Say:** God *(pause)* so loved the **world** *(pause)* that he gave his **only Son,** *(pause)* so that **everyone** *(pause)* who **believes** in him *(pause)* **won't perish** *(pause)* but will have **eternal life** (John 3:16).

Prepare

✓ Provide: heart puzzle made earlier (see page 17).

✓ Provide: masking tape.

Small Groups

Divide the children into small groups. You may organize the groups around age-levels or around readers and nonreaders. Keep the groups small, with a maximum of ten children in each group. You may need to have more than one of each group.

Young Children

- Show the children the Advent wreath.

- Point to first purple candle.

- **Say:** We light the first candle on the Advent wreath to help us remember hope.

- Light the first Advent candle.

- **Say:** We light the second candle on the Advent wreath to help us remember love. God so loved the world that he sent Jesus.

- Light the second Advent candle. Let the candles burn for a few minutes and then blow them out.

- Share the honey bread.

- Say a thank-you prayer.

- **Say:** Jesus is God's greatest gift of love. We can thank God for this gift of love by showing love to our families and friends.

- **Ask:** What are some ways that we can show love to our families and friends? (pray for them, give them hugs, say "I love you," share toys, share food and clothes, help with chores, and so forth)

- Give each child the bookmark pieces you cut out (page 24, top).

- Have the children color the two parts of their bookmarks. Let the children know that the bookmark has the name Jesus written on it.

- As the children are coloring, encourage each child to share one way they can show love to their families or friends.

- Give each child a piece of yarn about six to eight inches long.

- Show the children how to fold the two parts of their bookmarks in half.

- Have each child put glue on the inside of the fold and then place the yarn inside the fold as shown here.

- Have the child press firmly on both parts of the folded bookmark.

- Tell the children to place this bookmark in their Bibles at Luke 2.

- Read Luke 2:1-7 to the children.

- Close with prayer.

Prepare

- ✓ Set up an Advent wreath with four purple candles and one white candle.

- ✓ Provide: matches. (For adult use only. Keep the matches out of the children's reach.)

- ✓ Provide: the honey bread made earlier (page 17), and napkins.

- ✓ Photocopy the bookmark (page 24, top) for each child.

- ✓ Cut around each child's bookmark and on the solid lines and separate the small gift box on the right side.

- ✓ Cut yarn into six- to eight-inch lengths.

- ✓ Provide: crayons and glue.

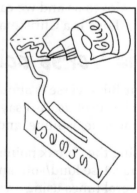

Art: Megan Jeffery
art © 2000 Abingdon Press

Older Children

- Show the children the Advent wreath.

- Point to first purple candle.

- **Say:** We light the first candle on the Advent wreath to help us remember hope.

- Light the first Advent candle.

- **Say:** We light the second candle on the Advent wreath to help us remember love. God so loved the world that he sent Jesus.

- Light the second Advent candle. Let the candles burn for a few minutes and then blow them out.

- Share the honey bread.

- Say a thank-you prayer.

- **Say:** In Jesus, God gave us the greatest gift possible, God's presence among us. This tells us how much God loves us. Let's say thank you to God by giving the gift of ourselves.

- Divide the children into pairs.

- **Ask:** How can you give a gift of yourself to God?

- Give the pairs two minutes to come up with the most creative way they can think of to "give a gift of themselves" to God.

- Have the pairs report.

- **Ask:** How can you give a gift of yourself to your family?

- Give the pairs two minutes to come up with the most creative way they can think of to "give a gift of themselves" to their families.

- Have the pairs report.

- **Ask:** How can you give a gift of yourself to others?

- Give the pairs two minutes to come up with the most creative way they can think of to "give a gift of themselves" to others.

- Have the pairs report.

- **Say:** Pick one of the ways of giving yourself to God, to your family, or to others that you would like to do this week.

- Give each child the large gift box (page 24, bottom).

- Have the children cut out the gift box.

- Encourage the children to write or draw a picture of the way of giving they chose in the gift box.

- Close with prayer.

Prepare

- ✓ Set up an Advent wreath with four purple candles and one white candle.

- ✓ Provide: matches. (For adult use only. Keep the matches out of the children's reach.)

- ✓ Provide: the honey bread made earlier (page 17) and napkins.

- ✓ Photocopy the large gift box (page 24, bottom) for each child.

- ✓ Provide: pencils, crayons, and safety scissors.

Art: Barbara Ball
art © 2004 Cokesbury

Christmas Gifts That Won't Break: Children's Leader Guide

Jesus Is Born

by LeeDell Stickler

(Trumpet sounds.) Give ear! Give ear! By order of the Emperor Augustus, all men will go to their hometown to be registered.

(Trumpet sounds.) And so Joseph went from Nazareth in Galilee to Judea, to the city of David called Bethlehem, because he was from the house and family of David. And he took with him Mary, who was expecting a child.

(Donkey hooves.) Up the hills and down the hills, the little donkey walked. *(Speed up and then slow down and speed up again.)* The sun was going down. Soon it would be night. *(Donkey hooves slower.)* Mary was tired. Joseph was tired, and the little donkey was even more tired. *(Donkey hooves even slower.)*

When the three came to the little town of Bethlehem, there was quite a crowd. *(Crowd sounds.)* The streets were filled with travelers. *(Crowd sounds.)* In fact, the city was so crowded that there was no place to stay.

Joseph went from house to house. *(Donkey hooves.)* He was looking for someplace—any place. But no one had any room. There was not an inch of floor space to be found anywhere.

Finally Joseph came to an inn. He knocked on the door. *(Door sounds.)*

The innkeeper opened the door. *(Crowd sounds.)*

"Go away!" said the innkeeper. "We have no room tonight!"

Joseph turned to go, pulling the little donkey behind him. *(Donkey hooves.)* The innkeeper saw Mary and the tired little donkey. He felt sorry for them.

"Wait. I have no room inside the inn. But I do have a stable where travelers keep their animals. You may sleep there tonight if you'd like," he said.

Joseph looked at Mary and then turned back to the innkeeper and nodded.

"Let me show you the way," the innkeeper said. *(Donkey hooves.)* The innkeeper led Mary and Joseph and the little donkey to a small stable.

The three looked around. It wasn't much, but there would be a roof over them tonight. And the animals would keep them company. *(Animal sounds.)*

Joseph laid his cloak across the hay. Mary lay down on it to rest. It had been a long journey.

(Animal sounds.) And that night, with only Joseph and the animals to keep her company *(soft animal sounds)*, Mary gave birth to baby Jesus. She wrapped him in bands of cloth and laid him in a manger where the animals ate. *(Animal sounds.)*

Baby Jesus, God's greatest gift of love to the world, was born in a stable because there was no room in the inn.

Adapted from BibleZone 2: Younger Elementary
© 1997 Abingdon Press

3 The Gift of Joy

Objectives

The children will
- hear Luke 2:8-12;
- discover that the good news about Jesus is a gift of joy;
- learn that Advent is a special time in the church year when we get ready to celebrate Jesus' birth;
- have the opportunity to experience the feeling of joy and share that feeling with others.

Bible Story

Luke 2:8-12: The angels tell the shepherds that a Savior is born.

Bible Verse

Luke 2:10: The angel said, "Don't be afraid! Look! I bring good news to you—wonderful, joyous news for all people."

Focus for the Teacher

The Shepherds' Story

The Scriptures tell us that angels filled the sky to announce the birth of God's Son. Angels in the Bible were powerful beings. Angels acted with God's authority and carried God's message. The word angel, derived from the Greek word *angelos*, means messenger.

Angels appearing to tell of Jesus' birth is not surprising. Such fanfare is appropriate for the birth of God's Son. But what is surprising is that they came to shepherds.

The religious leaders in the Jewish community looked down on the shepherds. Because of the very nature and difficulty of their work with the flocks, shepherds were not able to observe all the details of ceremonial law. For instance, it was impossible for them to follow all the rules and regulations of hand washing and food handling.

Yet the angels did go to the shepherds, reminding us that this gift of joy is for all people, both rich and poor.

> The angel said, "Don't be afraid! Look! I bring good news to you—wonderful, joyous news for all people."
> – Luke 2:10

The Bible Verse

Our Bible verse for today is the angel's message to the shepherds. A message of great joy for all the people—including you and me.

Celebrating Advent

This week you and your children will light the third purple candle on the Advent wreath. This candle helps us remember the third unbreakable gift, the gift of joy.

Be aware that for some of your children Christmas may be a time of stress rather than joy. The holidays can be a difficult time for children who have multiple families or no family at all. Talk with your pastor or children's director about any children you are concerned about.

Encourage your children to celebrate the unbreakable gift of joy. Help them focus on getting ready for Jesus' birth, not on the number of breakable gifts they will receive.

Christmas Gifts That Won't Break: Children's Leader Guide

Explore Interest Groups

Be sure that adult leaders are waiting when the first child arrives. Greet and welcome each child. Get the child involved in an activity that interests him or her and introduces the theme for the day's activities.

Shepherd's Staff Cookies (For All Ages)

- Have the children wash their hands.

- **Say:** Our Bible story for today begins with some shepherds out on a hillside watching their sheep. Shepherds often used staffs or crooks while they watched their sheep. Staffs were long wooden poles that had a curved hook on one end. The hook helped shepherds be able to pull a sheep out of a bush or off a rock. Let's make shepherd's staff cookies to share.

- Let the children work together to make the dough according to the recipe printed below. Or if you have a limited amount of time, prepare the dough before class.

- Give each child some dough and a piece of wax paper.

- Let the children roll the dough on the wax paper into a rope-like section. Advise them not to roll it too long or thin, or the cookie will break easily.

- Place the dough on an ungreased cookie sheet.

- Show the children how to curve one end into a shepherd's crook.

- Encourage the children to make several cookies. You will need a cookie for each child to eat as well as cookies to wrap and give away.

- Bake the cookies while the children are involved in other activities. Plan to eat the cookies during small group time.

Prepare

✓ Important: Be aware of food allergies the children may have before serving any recipe.

✓ Provide: ingredients, large mixing bowl, mixing spoon, measuring cups, measuring spoons, wax paper, cookie sheets, hand-washing supplies, and paper towels.

Shaping Dough

3 oz. package of cream cheese, softened
$1/2$ cup butter, softened
$1/2$ cup firmly packed brown sugar
$1/2$ teaspoon salt
1 teaspoon vanilla
$1^2/3$ cup all-purpose flour

Mix all ingredients except flour in a large bowl. Blend well by hand. Add flour. Stir until dough forms a ball. Knead on a floured surface, adding flour until dough is smooth and not sticky.

After shaping, bake at 350 degrees until lightly brown. Cool five minutes before removing from cookie sheet.

Wolf in the Sheepfold (For All Ages)

- Have the children move to an open area.

- **Say:** Today our Bible Story begins with some shepherds on a hillside. In biblical times sheep were important to a village. Not only did people use the wool to make clothing and blankets, but they also used the animal itself for food. So even though a shepherd was a lowly citizen of the village, his or her job was very important. One of the shepherd's main jobs was to protect the sheep. In this game, the shepherd needs to protect the sheep from a wolf.

- Select one child to be the shepherd and one child to be the wolf. The rest of the children will be the sheep.

- Have the sheep line up behind the shepherd. Each sheep will hold onto the shoulders of the child in front of him or her.

- The wolf will have its hungry eye on the sheep at the end of the line.

- **Say:** When I say, "go," the wolf is going to try to catch the lamb at the end of the line. If the wolf is able to grab onto the waist of the lamb, then the lamb is lamb chops. It'll be up to the shepherd and all the other sheep to protect the little lamb without letting go of one another. When the lamb is caught, the wolf takes it back to its den. The next-to-last person becomes the wolf's dinner prospect.

- Play until all the lambs have been caught.

- **Say:** A shepherd's job was very hard, but people often looked down on them. I wonder why God chose them to be the very first to hear the good news about Jesus' birth.

Adapted from Exploring Faith: Middle Elementary, Teacher Winter 2000-01 © 2000 Cokesbury

Golden Halos (For Younger Children)

- Show the children the biblical art you have collected.

- **Say:** For thousands of years people have created beautiful works of art based on Jesus' birth. The artists wanted these works of art to show that the angels, Mary and Joseph, and baby Jesus were good and holy. So some artists gave halos to these Bible characters. The halos were often made of real gold. A sheet of gold was pounded until it was very thin. The sheet was called gold leaf. The artist would stick the gold leaf onto the painting.

- Have the children wear paint smocks.

- Give each child a piece of dark-colored construction paper, a precut whole circle and a precut large triangle.

- **Say:** Our Bible story today tells how angels came to some shepherds to tell them the good news that baby Jesus was born.

- **Ask:** How would you feel if an angel suddenly appeared to you? Would you be afraid? How do you think the shepherds felt?

Prepare

✓ Cover the table with newspaper or plastic.

✓ Provide: dark-colored construction paper (purple, black, dark blue), gold wrapping paper, silver aluminum foil, glue, safety scissors, pencils, tempera paints, brushes, paint smocks, paper towels, and hand-washing supplies.

✓ Photocopy the shapes on page 34. For each child: cut the whole circle and the large triangle from construction paper; cut the half circle from gold wrapping paper; and cut the smaller triangles from silver wrapping paper or aluminum foil.

✓ Find artwork that shows gold leaf work in art books like the work of Fra Angelico. Some images are also available online:

http://www.christusrex .org/www2/art/beato.htm

http://www.christusrex .org/www2/art/images /beato05.jpg

Christmas Gifts That Won't Break: Children's Leader Guide

- **Say:** At first the shepherds were afraid, but their fear turned to joy when they heard the angel's message.

- Show the children how to arrange the circle and large triangle to make the angel's head and body. Help them glue the pieces in place.

- Give a half circle of gold wrapping paper and two small triangles of silver aluminum foil or wrapping paper to each child.

- Help the children glue the gold half circles in place to be the angels' halos and the silver triangles to be the angels' wings.

- Encourage the children to decorate their angels with tempera paint.

- Let the paintings dry.

Golden Halos (For Older Children)

- Show the children some of the biblical art you have collected.

- **Say:** For thousands of years people have created beautiful works of art based on the story of Jesus' birth. The artists wanted these works of art to show that the angels, Mary and Joseph, and baby Jesus were good and holy. So some artists gave golden halos to these Bible characters. The halos were often made of real gold. A sheet of gold was pounded until it was very thin. The thin sheet was called gold leaf. The artist would stick the gold leaf onto the painting.

- Have the children wear paint smocks.

- Give each child a piece of dark-colored construction paper.

- **Say:** Our Bible story today tells how angels came to some shepherds to tell them the good news that baby Jesus was born.

- **Ask:** How would you feel if an angel suddenly appeared to you? Would you be afraid? Would you be surprised? How do you think the shepherds felt?

- **Say:** At first the shepherds were afraid, but their fear turned to joy when they heard the angel's message.

- Encourage each child to draw a picture of an angel.

- Have each child choose a piece of gold or silver paper or foil.

- Let the children cut the gold and silver paper to fit one or two of the smaller areas of their drawings. For instance, a child might cut a gold halo for the angel's head or put silver stripes on the angel's wings. Encourage the children to use their imaginations.

- Have the children glue the gold or silver pieces to the drawings.

- Encourage the children to paint around the gold or silver areas with tempera paint.

- Let the paintings dry.

Prepare

✓ Cover the table with newspaper or plastic.

✓ Provide: blue or purple construction paper, small pieces of gold wrapping paper, silver wrapping paper or aluminum foil, glue, safety scissors, pencils, tempera paints, brushes, paint smocks, paper towels, and hand-washing supplies.

✓ Find artwork that shows gold leaf work in art books like the work of Fra Angelico. Some images are also available online:

http://www.christusrex.org/www2/art/beato.htm

http://www.christusrex.org/www2/art/images/beato05.jpg

Adapted from PowerXpress! The Gift of Jesus © 2001 Abingdon Press

Large Group

Bring all the children together to experience the Bible story. Ring jingle bells to alert the children to the large group time. Use the transition activity to move the children from the interest groups to the large group area.

Angel Relay

- Divide the children into teams.
- Have the teams move to one side of the room.
- Place a stuffed sheep on the opposite side of the room for each team.
- Place angel wings and a halo on the floor in front of each team.
- **Say:** When baby Jesus was born, there were shepherds keeping watch over their sheep. Suddenly an angel appeared to the shepherds and told them about Mary's baby. Each of you will have a chance to be that angel. When I say, "go," the first person in line will put on the angel wings and halo and then run across the room to the stuffed sheep. Then the angel will pick up the sheep and shout, "I've got good news!" Then put down the stuffed sheep. Finally, the angel will run back to his or her team and give the wings and halo to the next person in line.
- Make sure everyone understands the relay and then say, "Go!"
- Continue the relay until every child has a turn.
- Encourage the children to hum "Away in a Manger" as they sit down in the large group area.

Advent Acts

- Present the drama "The Shepherds' Amazing Story" (page 35) to the children.
- **Say:** Everybody look up. (Have the children look up.)
- **Ask:** How would you feel if you looked up into the sky and saw angels? The shepherds were afraid. Would you be afraid?
- **Say:** The angels told the shepherds that they had news of great joy.
- **Ask:** What kind of news would make you feel joy?
- Have the children turn to the person next to them and answer the question. After a few minutes, invite the children to share some of their answers with the large group.
- **Say:** Those things can make us feel joy. But the message the angels gave the shepherds was even better than those things. The angels had the best news ever. The angels told the shepherds that the Messiah, God's Son, was born. It was news of great joy!

Prepare

✓ Place a stuffed sheep on one side of the room for each team.

✓ Provide: angel wings and a halo for each team.

Prepare

✓ Recruit older children, youths, or adults to be the 3 shepherds, the angel, and the narrator.

✓ Photocopy the drama (page 35) for the actors.

Optional

✓ Provide costumes for the characters.

✓ Set up the large group stage area to be a hillside or field. Place real or artificial plants around the area. Place stuffed sheep around the plants.

✓ Add a pretend campfire. Turn on a flashlight and place it on the floor. Pile sticks or blocks of wood to hide the flashlight and make the campfire. Stuff red and yellow tissue paper or cellophane among the pieces of wood.

Word Play

- Divide the children into teams of four or five children. Have the teams move to one side of the room.

- **Ask:** Have you ever seen a football game?

- **Say:** When the football teams runs out onto the field, the crowd cheers for their team.

- **Ask:** How do you think that makes the football players feel? Excited? happy? joyful?

- **Say:** Let's try it and see.

- Roll out one of the joy banners.

- **Ask:** What does this say? *(joy)*

- Have two adults or older children hold each side of the banner. Spread the banner across the middle of the room. Make sure there is open space behind the banner.

- Choose a team to be first. Have the other teams stand away from the banner.

- **Say:** Let's all cheer for this team as they run through the banner.

- Let the team break through the banner while the other children cheer.

- Repeat the process for each team.

- **Say:** The angel's message to the shepherds is a message of joy for us today. God's Son was born for each one of us.

Bible Verse Sing-a-long

- Have the children sit down in your large group area.

- Open a Bible to Luke 2.

- **Say:** Our Bible verse today is Luke 2:10, "The angel said, 'Don't be afraid! Look! I bring good news to you—wonderful, joyous news for all people.'" Let's sing some songs based on this Bible verse.

London Bridge

See, I'm bringing you good news,
you good news, you good news.
See, I'm bringing you good news,
of great joy.

Row, Row, Row, Your Boat

See, I'm bringing you,
bringing you good news,
I am bringing you good news
of great joy today.

Did You Ever See a Lassie?

Did you ever see an angel,
an angel, an angel?
Did you ever see an angel
bringing good news?
Good news of great joy,
O good news of great joy.
Did you ever see an angel
bringing good news?

Prepare

- ✓ Make banners from mural paper for each team.

- ✓ Use wide markers to write the word joy in large letters across the banner.

Small Groups

Divide the children into small groups. You may organize the groups around age-levels or around readers and nonreaders. Keep the groups small, with a maximum of ten children in each group. You may need to have more than one of each group.

Young Children

- Show the children the Advent wreath.

- **Say:** We light the first candle on the Advent wreath to help us remember hope.

- Light the first Advent candle.

- **Say:** We light the second candle on the Advent wreath to help us remember love.

- Light the second Advent candle.

- **Say:** We light the third candle on the Advent wreath to help us remember joy. The angels told the shepherds good news of great joy—God's Son is born.

- Light the third Advent candle. Let the candles burn for a few minutes and then blow them out.

- Share the shepherd staff cookies. Say a thank-you prayer.

- **Say:** Like the angel, we can share God's message of joy with others.

- Give each child a small container with a lid.

- Let the children tear colored tissue paper into small pieces.

- Have the children glue the tissue paper onto the containers. Let the children to completely cover the containers with the tissue paper.

- Pour white glue into shallow containers and thin with water. Show the children how to use the brushes to paint the glue over the tissue paper. Encourage the children to completely cover the containers.

- Give each child the strips of Bible verses that you cut apart before small group time. If you have children who can cut, they can cut apart the verse themselves.

- Have each child place the Bible verses inside the containers and close the lids.

- **Say:** These jars are filled with Bible verses that help us remember God's message of joy. You may give these jars for a friend or family member. They can open the jar and pick out one of the Bible verses to read whenever they wish.

- Open a container and pull out one of the Bible verses. Read the verse to the children.

- Close with prayer.

Prepare

- ✓ Set up an Advent wreath with four purple candles and one white candle.

- ✓ Provide: matches. (For adult use only. Keep the matches out of the children's reach.)

- ✓ Provide: small unbreakable containers with lids for each child. These may be plastic jars, coffee cans, potato chip cans, or gift boxes. If the containers have writing on the outside, let the children use fabric scraps instead of tissue paper. Precut fabric into small pieces.

- ✓ Photocopy and cut apart the Bible verses (page 65) for each child.

- ✓ Provide: scissors, colored tissue paper, white glue, water, glue brushes, and shallow containers.

Christmas Gifts That Won't Break: Children's Leader Guide

Older Children

- Show the children the Advent wreath.

- **Say:** We light the first candle on the Advent wreath to help us remember hope.

- Light the first Advent candle.

- **Say:** We light the second candle on the Advent wreath to help us remember love.

- Light the second Advent candle.

- **Say:** We light the third candle on the Advent wreath to help us remember joy. The angels told the shepherds good news of great joy—God's Son is born!

- Light the third Advent candle. Let the candles burn for a few minutes and then blow them out.

- Share the shepherd staff cookies. Say a thank-you prayer.

- **Say:** Like the angel, we can share God's message of joy with others.

- Give each child a small container with a lid.

- Let the children tear colored tissue paper into small pieces or cut fabric scraps into small pieces.

- Have the children glue the tissue paper or fabric scraps onto the container. Encourage the children to completely cover the containers.

- Have each child use a dark permanent marker to write the word joy on the covered container.

- Pour white glue into shallow containers and thin with water. Let the children use brushes to paint over the tissue paper or fabric. Encourage the children to completely cover the containers.

- Have each child cut the strips of Bible verses apart.

- Have the children place the Bible verses inside the containers.

- Instruct the children to close the lids.

- **Say:** These containers are filled with Bible verses that help us remember God's message of joy. You may give these to a friend or family member. They can open the containers and pick out one of the Bible verses to read whenever they wish.

- Have each child open a container and pull out one of the Bible verses.

- Encourage each child to read the verse to the group.

- Close with prayer.

Prepare

✓ Set up an Advent wreath with four purple candles and one white candle.

✓ Provide: matches. (For adult use only. Keep the matches out of the children's reach.)

✓ Provide: small unbreakable containers with lids for each child. These may be plastic jars, coffee cans, potato chip cans, or gift boxes. If the containers have writing on the outside, let the children use fabric scraps instead of tissue paper.

✓ Photocopy the Bible verses (page 65) for each child.

✓ Provide: safety scissors, colored tissue paper or fabric scraps, white glue, water, glue brushes, shallow containers, and dark-colored permanent markers.

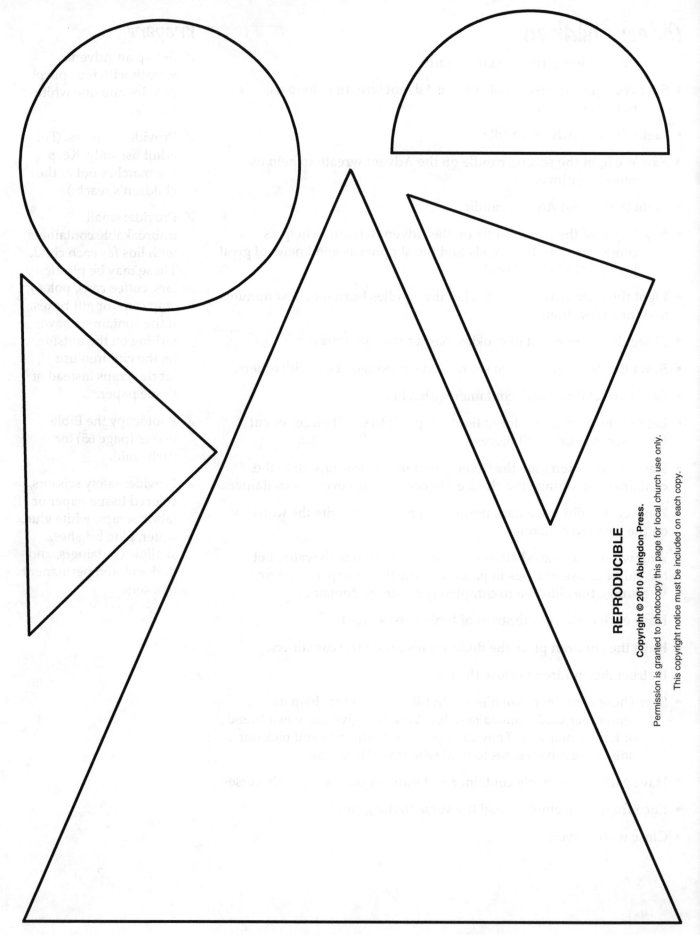

The Shepherds' Amazing Story

by Valerie A. Foster

Larry: Six hundred and sixty-six, six hundred and sixty-seven . . .

Jarrel: Sheep, sheep, sheep. I'm sick of sheep! I wish I had I never taken this job.

Larry: I know what you mean! All I wanted was a little adventure. You know—fighting off wolves and seeing the world. Some world! All I see is green grass and hundreds of sheep.

Jarrel: And the smell *(holding his nose)*. Phew! Who knew sheep smelled so bad?

Harry: *(taking a deep breath)* I don't know. I kind of like it. Peace and quiet. *(laying back and folding his arms behind his head)* Plenty of rest. *(patting stuffed sheep)* The sheep aren't so much trouble.

Jarrel: Peace and quiet! No trouble! How can you get any rest with them BAA, BAA, BAAing all the time? It drives me crazy!

Harry: But just look at that sky. It's so beautiful! What could be better than that?

Jarrel: All I see is a black sky covered with millions of white dots. What's so great about that?

Larry: Yeah, it's the same sky we see night after night after night.

Narrator: While the shepherds were arguing out in the fields, a man named Joseph and his fiancée, Mary, were traveling to Bethlehem. Emperor Augustus wanted all people to be registered in their hometowns. Since he was the Emperor, everyone had to listen to him! When Mary and Joseph got to Bethlehem, the city was overflowing with people, and they couldn't find a place to stay. Joseph was really worried because Mary was expecting a baby. Finally, they found room in a stable. Being very tired, they made their bed amongst the animals. Back in the fields, the shepherds were still complaining when, suddenly, a brilliant light filled the dark sky. Terrified, they buried their heads in their hands.

Larry: *(fearfully)* What's happening?

Jarrel: *(crying)* It's the end of the world!

Harry: God, please help us!

Narrator: Suddenly, an angel of the Lord appeared before them and said . . .

Angel: Don't be afraid. I have great news. The Messiah is born! You will find him in Bethlehem, lying in a manger.

Narrator: The sky filled with angels praising God. Then as suddenly as they appeared, the angels were gone.

Larry: *(shaking his head)* Uh, did anyone else see what I just saw?

Jarrel: 'Course we saw it! We're not blind!

Larry: *(shrugging his shoulders)* OK, OK! I was just checking!

Harry: Amazing! Can you believe God sent angels down to us? Three worthless shepherds. And now, WOW! God chose to tell us the news of the century! COME ON, LET'S GO!

Jarrel and Larry: *(speaking at same time)* Go? Go where?

Harry: *(sighing)* To Bethlehem, of course, to the city of David. To see the Messiah!

Adapted from BibleZone 2, Older Elementary, Teacher's Guide. © 1997 Abingdon Press.

Lesson 3: The Gift of Joy

4 The Gift of Peace

<table>
<tr><td>

Objectives

The children will
- hear Luke 2:8-20;
- discover that the good news about Jesus is a gift of peace;
- learn that Advent is a special time when we get ready to celebrate Jesus' birth;
- have the opportunity to explore what it means to live in peace.

</td><td>

Bible Story

Luke 2:8-20: The shepherds find baby Jesus.

Bible Verse

Luke 2:14, CEV: "Praise God in heaven! Peace on earth to everyone who pleases God."

</td></tr>
</table>

Focus for the Teacher

The Angels' Song

After the angel made the announcement to the shepherds the sky was filled with angels, praising God and singing, "Praise God in heaven! Peace on earth to everyone who pleases God" (Luke 2:14, CEV).

In the Bible, peace means more than "no fighting." The Hebrew word *shalom* means wholeness, well-being, and rightness with God. In fact, peace and salvation are related words. God is described as the God of peace; the Messiah is called the Prince of Peace who will usher in an age where all creation lives in harmony. The angels were singing about this kind of peace.

> "Praise God in heaven! Peace on earth to everyone who pleases God."
> –Luke 2:14, CEV

The shepherds were not only the first to hear the good news, but they were also the first to respond by seeking Jesus and telling others the good news. The shepherds "returned, glorifying and praising God." How will you return to your daily life after Christmas? By teaching these lessons, you have the opportunity to praise God and tell the good news. Pray that God will work through you to reach others with the good news.

The Bible Verse

Our Bible verse is part of the angel's visit to the shepherds. A host of angels appears, singing and praising God. The verse reminds us that the birth of God's Son brings peace.

Celebrating Advent

This week you and your children will light the fourth purple candle on the Advent wreath as you remember the gift of peace.

At Christmas, the Christ-child comes into the world as the Prince of Peace. He brings the peace that we are called to pass on to others.

Hope, Love, Joy, and Peace...

These are the Christmas gifts that always fit. These are the Christmas gifts that never go out of style. These are the Christmas gifts wrapped in heaven. These are the Christmas gifts that we as Christian disciples are called upon to pass on to others. These are the Christmas gifts that won't break!

—James W. Moore

Explore Interest Groups

Be sure that adult leaders are waiting when the first child arrives. Greet and welcome each child. Get the child involved in an activity that interests him or her and introduces the theme for the day's activities.

A Multitude of Angels (For All Ages)

- Let the children choose one or more ways to create angels. Display the angels all around your room to create a multitude.

- **Say:** On the night that Jesus was born, the shepherds saw not one angel, not two angels, but a multitude of angels in the sky. That's a lot of angels. Let's see how many angels we can add to our room today.

Angel Garlands

- Have the older children cut out two of the angels.

- Give younger children two precut angels.

- Encourage each child to decorate the two angels to be him or herself.

- **Say:** I wonder what it would be like to be an angel.

- **Ask:** What do you think you would do all day? How do you think it would feel to sing praise to God?

- **Say:** We don't have to be angels to praise God. Let's make these angels to look like ourselves to help us remember that we can praise God, too.

- When the children have finished their angels, stretch out a string or piece of yarn across the room.

- Have the children put glue on one of the angels and sandwich the string between the angel with the glue and the angel without the glue.

- Hang the garland in your large group area.

Adapted from Exploring Faith: Middle Elementary, Teacher, Winter 2006–07 © 2006 Cokesbury

Glittering Angel Prints

- Have older children cut out the sandpaper angel pattern.

- Instruct the older children to place the angel cutout on the back (smooth side) of a sheet of sandpaper. Let the children trace the angel and then cut around the outline.

- Give younger children the precut sandpaper angels.

- Encourage the children to use metallic crayons to color the front (rough side) of their angels.

Prepare

✓ Photocopy at least two copies of the multitude of angels pattern (page 47) for each child.

✓ Cut out at least two copies of the angel for each younger child.

✓ Provide: paper, crayons or markers, string or yarn, safety scissors, and glue.

Prepare

✓ Photocopy the sandpaper angel pattern (page 46) for each child.

✓ Precut angels from the sandpaper for younger children.

✓ Provide: sandpaper (any texture), pencils, metallic crayons, old newspapers, ironing board and iron, black construction paper, and safety scissors.

- Cover an ironing board with newspaper. Place each sandpaper angel face-down on a sheet of black construction paper. (This step must be done with adult supervision only.) Set the iron on medium heat. Lightly press the back side of the sandpaper.

- The metallic crayon design will transfer to the black construction paper in tiny dots.

- Display the prints around the room.

Adapted from Exploring Faith: Middle Elementary, Teacher, Winter 2006–07 © 2006 Cokesbury

Origami Angel
(For Older Children)

- Help the children follow these instructions to create origami angels:

1. Make a fold two inches down from the four-inch edge of one piece of foil.
2. Fold again so that you have a double flap that is two inches long.
3. Unfold the paper.
4. Fold the left corner down even with the right side.
5. Fold the right corner down to the left so that it matches the left-hand fold.
6. Open the folds.
7. Refold the top edge to make a single two-inch flap.
8. Fold each of the top corners inside to create a triangle at the top of the foil rectangle.
9. Fold the left corner of the triangle to the right.
10. Fold the left side of the paper from the left-hand point down the center line.
11. Fold both corners of the triangle back to the left side.
12. Fold the right side of the paper from the right-hand point down the center line.
13. Unfold the right corner of the triangle piece.
14. Turn the angel over.
15. Fold the point at the top of the angel toward the front to create the head.

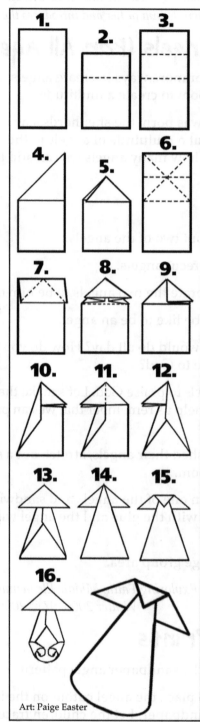

Art: Paige Easter

Prepare
✓ Provide: foil wrapping paper, safety scissors, and tape.

✓ Cut two 4- by 8-inch rectangles of foil wrapping paper for each child.

✓ Practice making the angel. Use your angel as a sample to show the children.

16. Curl the sides at the bottom of the angel to the back to shape it. Put a small piece of tape at the bottom to hold the shape.

- Display the angels around the room.

- Have the children make a second angel to give away. Encourage them to tell the person who receives the angel the messages that angels brought to Mary, Joseph, and the shepherds.

Adapted from PowerXpress! Christmas Messengers © 2007 Abingdon Press

Life-sized Angel (For Younger Children)

Prepare
✓ Provide: mural paper, scissors, crayons, and tape.

- Have the children find partners. If you have an uneven number of children, be a child's partner.

- Give each pair of children two pieces of mural paper the length of each child's height.

- Have the children spread the papers out flat on the floor.

- Have one child lie on a length of paper with his or her arms outstretched.

- Have the partner trace around the child's head, arms, and upper body.

- Ask the partner to draw lines down the paper to form an angel's robe.

- Then have the partners reverse positions so that the other child's outline can be drawn on the other piece of mural paper.

- Encourage the children to use crayons or markers to color the hair, eyes, and features of their angels to be just like themselves.

- Display the angels around the room.

Adapted from PowerXpress! The Gift of Jesus © 2001 Abingdon Press

Wandering Sheep (For All Ages)

- Divide the children into two groups.

- Have the teams stand on either side of a boundary line.

- **Say:** Shepherds had to constantly watch their sheep to make sure they did not wander away. One person from each team is going to pretend to be a wandering sheep. The sheep cross the other team's boundary line. Once across the line, the sheep have to make a BAAing sound in one breath. While they are BAAing, the sheep try to tag as many players as they can. Once they run out of breath, they have to stop and go back to their side of the boundary. Any players that are tagged are out of the game. If another player grabs the BAAing sheep from behind and holds him or her until they run out of breath, all those that were tagged are free and that player is out of the game.

- Make sure the children understand the game and then start to play.

Lesson 4: The Gift of Peace

Large Group

Bring all the children together to experience the Bible story. Ring jingle bells to alert the children to the large group time. Use the transition activity to move the children from the interest groups to the large group area.

Shepherd Shuffle (For All Ages)

- Divide the children into teams. Have the teams go to one side of the room.

- Place a small Nativity scene or a picture of the Nativity inside a box for each team. Set the boxes on the opposite side of the room.

- **Say:** When the angels vanished, the shepherds hurried to Bethlehem to find baby Jesus. After they saw the baby, the shepherds told everyone they met the good news that God's Son was born. The goal of this game is to hurry to Bethlehem to see the new baby. Only this is the way you must travel.

- Show the children how to put each foot into a shoebox and shuffle across the room.

- **Say:** When you get to the box across the room, look in the box to see what's there. Then shuffle back to the next person in line and tell them what you saw.

- Place two shoeboxes at the beginning of each team's line. Make sure everyone understands the relay and then say, "Go!"

- Continue the relay until every child has a turn.

- Encourage the children to hum "Away in a Manger" as they sit down in the large group area.

Prepare
- ✓ Place a Nativity or Nativity picture inside a box on one side of the room for each team.

- ✓ Provide: two shoeboxes for each team.

Advent Acts

- Have the children stay seated in the large group area, but scoot around until there is space between each child.

- Tell the story, "Going on a Journey, Got to Find the Baby" (pages 44–45) to the children. Encourage the children to participate.

- **Ask:** What did the angels tell the shepherds? What did the shepherds do when the angels went away? How do you think the shepherds felt when they saw baby Jesus?

Prepare
- ✓ Photocopy "Going on a Journey, Got to Find the Baby" (pages 44–45).

Word Play

- **Say:** Everyone stand up. I'm going to play some music. While the music is playing, I will hit five balloons out to you. I want you to stay quiet and hit the balloons back and forth to each other the whole time the music plays. When the music stops, I want whoever is holding a balloon to stay standing. I want anyone who is not holding a balloon to sit down. Remember, no talking.

Prepare
- ✓ Blow up five balloons. Write one of the letters in the word peace on each balloon using permanent markers.

- Start playing quiet Christmas music ("Silent Night," "Away in a Manger," "O Little Town of Bethlehem," "What Child Is This?" and so forth).

- Hit the five balloons out to the children. Encourage them to keep the balloons moving back and forth among the children. Remind them to keep silent.

- Stop the music. Have the five children holding the balloons remain standing and everyone else sit down.

- Have the children holding the five balloons come to the front.

- **Say:** Look. Each of the balloons has a letter. Please hold the balloons so everyone can see the letters.

- **Ask:** What word do you think this spells?

- Help the children arrange themselves so that the letters spell the word *peace*.

- **Say:** Peace. The angels sang praise to God and promised peace on earth. Peace is a Christmas gift that will not break.

Prepare
✓ Provide: CD with quiet Christmas music, and a CD player.

Bible Verse Two-Step (For All Ages)

- Have the children line up across the play area. If you have a large number of children, divide the children into teams.

- Give each child the two Bible verse pages.

- Hold up a copy of the first page. Say the first part of the Bible verse for the children.

- Hold up a copy of the second page. Say the second part of the Bible verse for the children.

- **Say:** Repeat each part of the Bible verse when I hold up its page.

- Hold up page one, then page two. Have the children repeat the verse when they see the pages.

- Vary how you hold up the pages. Hold up page one twice in a row, then page two. Hold up page two and then page one.

- **Say:** Now, let's play a game with our verse. Place the two Bible pages on the floor. When I say "go," everyone will step on the first Bible page with one foot. While you are still standing on one foot, bend over and pick up the second page. Set it on the floor ahead of you and step on it with one foot. Then pick up the first page and do the same thing. The object is to get to the finish line by stepping on the Bible verse pages without stepping on the floor. If you step on the floor, you must go back to the starting line and start again.

- Make sure the children understand the game and then say, "go!"

Prepare
✓ Write "Praise God in heaven!" in large letters on a sheet of copy paper. On a second sheet, write "Peace on earth to everyone who pleases God." Photocopy the two pages for each child. Keep one copy for the leader.

✓ Use masking tape to mark a starting line and a finish line.

Small Groups

Divide the children into small groups. You may organize the groups around age-levels or around readers and nonreaders. Keep the groups small, with a maximum of ten children in each group. You may need to have more than one of each group.

Young Children

- Show the children the Advent wreath.

- **Say:** We light the first candle on the Advent wreath to help us remember hope.

- Light the first Advent candle.

- **Say:** We light the second candle on the Advent wreath to help us remember love.

- Light the second Advent candle.

- **Say:** We light the third candle on the Advent wreath to help us remember joy.

- Light the third Advent candle.

- **Say:** We light the fourth candle on the Advent wreath to help us remember peace. When Jesus was born, a multitude of angels sang praise to God and promised peace on earth.

- Light the fourth Advent candle. Let the candles burn for a few minutes and then blow them out.

- **Ask:** What are some things we can do to help there be peace on earth? (stop fighting; help others; love God, ourselves, and others; be kind; show love to people who are different than us)

- **Say:** Peace is a Christmas gift that won't break. The angels promised peace on earth to the shepherds. We can share the angel's message with others. Peace is a blessing we can offer to others, and it is a blessing God offers to us.

- Use a small amount of clear lip balm to make a "P" or a cross on the forehead or the back of a hand of each child.

- **Say:** (Child's name), you are a blessing from God to us all. Share your blessings and gifts with other people.

- Close with a prayer.

Prepare

✓ Set up an Advent wreath with four purple candles and one white candle.

✓ Provide: clear lip balm and matches. (For adult use only. Keep the matches out of the children's reach.)

Older Children

- Show the children the Advent wreath.

- **Say:** We light the first candle on the Advent wreath to help us remember hope.

- Light the first Advent candle.

- **Say:** We light the second candle on the Advent wreath to help us remember love.

- Light the second Advent candle.

- **Say:** We light the third candle on the Advent wreath to help us remember joy.

- Light the third Advent candle.

- **Say:** We light the fourth candle on the Advent wreath to help us remember peace. When Jesus was born, a multitude of angels sang praise to God and promised peace on earth.

- Light the fourth Advent candle. Let the candles burn for a few minutes and then blow them out.

- **Ask:** What are some things we can do to help there be peace on earth? (stop fighting; help others; love God, ourselves, and others, be kind, show love to people who are different than us)

- **Say:** Peace is a Christmas gift that won't break. The angels promised peace on earth to the shepherds. We can share the angel's message with others. Peace is a blessing we can offer to others, and it is a blessing God offers to us.

- Use a small amount of clear lip balm to make a "P" or a cross on the forehead or the back of a hand of each child.

- **Say:** (Child's name), you are a blessing from God to us all. Share your blessings and gifts with other people.

- Close with a prayer.

Prepare

✓ Set up an Advent wreath with four purple candles and one white candle.

✓ Provide: clear lip balm and matches. (For adult use only. Keep the matches out of the children's reach.)

Going on a Journey, Got to Find the Baby

by Suzann Wade

Instruct the children to imitate your actions. Whenever you say, "Going on a Journey," the children respond with "Got to Find the Baby." Practice this response before starting the story.

It's nighttime and all is quiet and still. We are watching our flocks in the fields. *(Cup hands on either side of your eyes as if looking at something.)*

Suddenly, a bright light appears in the sky. *(Cover your eyes as if shielding them from a bright light.)*

A voice speaks. *(Put your hand to your ear.)*

It is an angel, telling us about a baby, the Savior, the Messiah. A choir is singing praises to God and promising peace. Then just as suddenly, the angels are gone.

We know what we have to do; we have to find that baby.

Going on a journey, got to find the baby.

We jump to our feet. *(Jump to your feet.)*

We run across the field. *(Run in place.)*

Look out! There are the sheep. It's too far to go around them; we better go through them.

Going on a journey, got to find the baby.

Here we go, zigzagging through the sheep. *(Move from side to side as if dodging sheep.)*

Oh no! Lambs! Hurry! Jump over them! *(Jump as if jumping a hurdle.)*

Big sheep! Lots of big sheep. *(Move from side to side again.)* More lambs! Lots of lambs. *(Jump again.)*

Whew! We're through the sheep. *(Act as if you are trying to catch your breath.)*

But we can't stop too long.

Going on a journey, got to find the baby.

Look! I see lights up ahead. *(Hold your hand up by your eyes.)*

Uh-oh! Hills. We can't go under them. We can't go around them. We've got to go over them.

Going on a journey, got to find the baby.

We are at the bottom of the first hill. *(Squat down and look up as if looking up the hill.)*

Up, up, up we go. *(Raise up a little each time you say the word up, until you are standing.)*

Up to the very top. *(Stretch and reach up as you raise up on your toes.)*

We're at the top of the first hill.

Now, down we go. *(Bring your hands down to normal standing position.)* Down, down, down the hill. *(Lower down a little each time you say the word down.)*

We're at the bottom of the first hill. *(Squat back down.)*

Going on a journey, got to find the baby.

Let's get up and run across the valley. *(Run in place.)*

Now, we're at the bottom of the second hill. *(Squat down and look up as if looking up the hill.)*

OK, up, up, up we go. *(Raise up a little each time you say the word up, until you are standing.)*

Up to the very top. *(Stretch and reach up as you raise up on your toes.)*

We're at the top of the second hill.

Now, down we go. *(Bring hands down to normal standing.)* Down, down, down the hill. *(Lower down a little each time you say the word down.)*

We're at the bottom of the second hill. *(Squat back down.)*

The town is straight ahead. We run into town. *(Run in place.)*

We're looking for a manger. We've got to find the manger.

Going on a journey, got to find the baby.

Hurry let's check all the stables. We run from stable to stable looking in each one. (*Run back and forth from side to side several times, stopping on each side to act as if opening a door and looking inside a building.*)

No babies here.

Look! Up ahead, there's a light on in that stable, let's go see. (*Run in place.*)

Wait! (*Hold up your hand and stop.*)

Listen! (*Put your hand to your ear.*)

It's a baby. There's a baby crying in there. This must be it!

How do we look? Do we look OK? (*Motion as if fixing your headdress and clothes.*)

Shhh! (*Hold up a finger to your lips.*)

We better be quiet.

(*Whisper.*) **Going on a journey, got to find the baby.**

Let's go inside. (*Motion opening the door.*)

Look! There's the baby. (*Look surprised and cover your mouth with both hands.*)

Mary and Joseph ask us to come closer. We've found him. We found the Messiah!

Let us worship and give thanks to God. (*Kneel and hold your hands in prayer.*)

Now, it is time for us to go back to our flocks. (*Stand.*)

We leave the beautiful family to head back to our fields.

But first, we must tell everyone the good news. (*Run back and forth from side to side, stopping on each side to act as if opening a door. Cup your hand to your mouth to motion calling inside.*)

Now, the whole town has heard our cries. Back to our fields, friends. I'm so excited I could run all the way back. (*Run in place.*)

We're at the bottom of the first hill (*Squat down.*)

Up we go! (*Do all of the motions going up very fast until you are stretched up on your toes.*)

We're at the top of the hill.

Now, down we go! (*Do all the motions of going down very fast until you are squatting again.*)

Across the valley! (*Run in place.*)

We're back at the second hill. (*Squat down.*)

Up we go! (*Do all the motions of going up very fast until you are stretched up on your toes.*)

We're at the top of the hill.

Now, down we go! (*Do all the motions of going down very fast until you are squatting again.*)

Across the field! (*Run in place.*)

Look out, lambs! (*Jump as if jumping over several hurdles.*)

Oh no, big sheep! (*Move from side to side as if dodging sheep.*)

More lambs! (*Jump as if jumping over several hurdles.*)

More big sheep! (*Move from side to side as if dodging sheep.*)

Whew, we're back. (*Stop as if trying to catch your breath.*)

We went on a journey!

We found the baby!

Good job, friends. Now, let's get some sleep. (*Fall on the ground and pretend to be sleeping.*)

Adapted from PowerXpress! Journey to Bethlehem © 2004 Abingdon Press

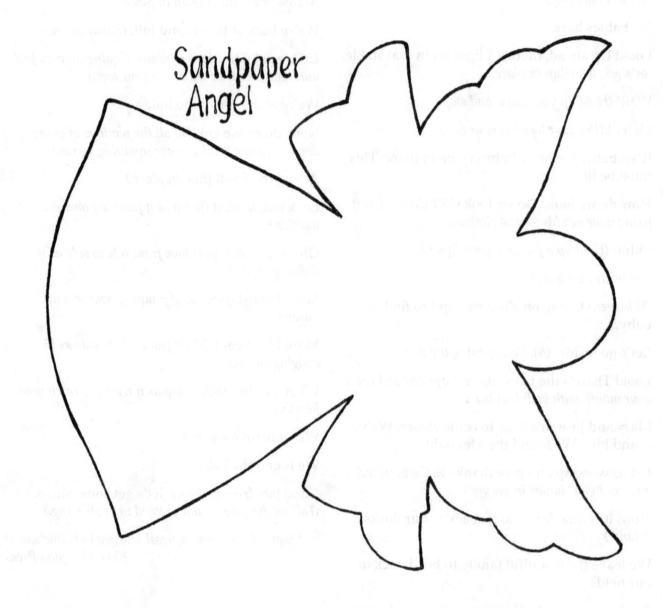

Sandpaper
Angel

Art: Barbara Ball
art © 2006 Cokesbury

Multitude of Angels

GLUE BACK TO RIBBON

DECORATE FRONT...GLUE OVER BACK

Ann

Joe

Ann

Justin

Jenny

Art: Barbara Ball
art © 2006 Cokesbury

REPRODUCIBLE

5 The Gift of Christ

Objectives

The children will
- hear Matthew 2:1-12;
- discover that the good news about the gift of Jesus;
- learn that Advent is a special time when we get ready to celebrate Jesus' birth;
- have the opportunity to explore what Christmas truly means.

Bible Story

Matthew 2:1-12: The magi follow the star to find Jesus.

Bible Verse

Matthew 2:10: When they saw the star, they were filled with joy.

Focus for the Teacher

The Magi's Journey

Today's story conveys the message that God sent Jesus to everyone. The magi were Gentiles, traveling from the East. They were non-Jews who came searching for a new king. The magi had not been waiting for the birth of a Messiah for hundreds of years as the Jews had. Rather, they came because they were astrologers who had seen a new star. They believed the appearance of the new star meant a king had been born, and they were curious. They followed the star, searching for this new king. When the star led them to a house in Bethlehem, the magi were "filled with joy."

Spend some time reflecting on the magi. God chose to send Jesus for everyone, even those who have not been waiting for his arrival and aren't fully aware of whom they are seeking. Like the magi, we receive the news of Jesus' birth with joy and honor him with gifts. Help your children to understand that although we cannot bring gifts to Jesus in person like the magi did, we can still honor Jesus with our gifts.

> When they saw the star, they were filled with joy.
>
> —Matthew 2:10

The Bible Verse

Our Bible verse is the magi's response to the star leading them to Jesus. The magi acted on their feelings of joy by worshipping Jesus and offering him gifts. What is your response to Jesus? Does the good news of Christ fill you with joy?

Celebrating Advent

This week you and your children will light the white center candle on the Advent wreath as you remember the gift of Christ.

Throughout Advent, we have celebrated the Christmas gifts that won't break represented by the outer candles of the Advent wreath: hope, love, joy, and peace. Now, we celebrate the greatest gift of all, represented by the center candle: the gift of Jesus Christ. Jesus really is what it's all about, what Christmas truly means. The gift of Jesus Christ is the gift of the very foundation of our faith.

—James W. Moore

Explore Interest Groups

Be sure that adult leaders are waiting when the first child arrives. Greet and welcome each child. Get the child involved in an activity that interests him or her and introduces the theme for the day's activities.

Painted Star Cookies (For All Ages)

- Refrigerate the purchased dough for 1-2 hours before the children arrive.

- Preheat the oven according to the directions on the package.

- Spray cookie sheets with nonstick spray.

- Cover work surface with wax paper and sprinkle with sugar.

- Roll cookie dough to 1/4 -inch thickness.

- Cut out star-shaped cookies.

- Place about a tablespoon of condensed milk in each of several small bowls. Add drops of food coloring to each bowl of milk to create food paint.

- Give the children clean brushes. Let the children paint the cookies with the food paint.

- **Say:** The magi were men who studied the star. On the night Jesus was born, a bright star appeared in the sky. The magi believed that the star meant a new king had been born. The magi followed the star to Bethlehem where they found Jesus. They worshiped Jesus with gifts of gold, frankincense, and myrrh.

- Bake the cookies according to directions.

- Let the cookies cool and save them for the closing party.

Imagining the Star (For All Ages)

- Show the children the star pictures (page 59).

- **Say:** No one knows which star guided the magi from the East to Bethlehem. Some say the star was undergoing an unusually bright phase in its life cycle. Others say the star may have actually been a comet. Still others say it was two planets appearing close together. Whatever the star looked like, we know it was not the five-point star we see in Christmas decorations. Here are some pictures of what some artists imagine the star might have looked like. Let's use our own imaginations.

- Invite the children to create paintings of the stars they imagined.

- **Ask:** Why was the star important to the magi? What are some ways that God continues to lead people to worship Jesus today?

Adapted from PowerXpress!®Bible Experience Stations® Follow the Star © 2006 Cokesbury

Prepare

✓ Important: Be aware of food allergies the children may have before serving any recipe.

✓ Provide: hand-washing supplies, purchased sugar cookie dough, cookie sheets, nonstick spray, rolling pin, small bowls, condensed milk, food coloring, tablespoon, wax paper, sugar, clean paint brushes, and star-shaped cookie cutters.

Prepare

✓ Photocopy at least one of the Star Pictures (page 59).

✓ Cover your work surfaces with paper or plastic.

✓ Provide: table covering, paper, washable paint, paint smocks, and brushes.

A van Gogh Christmas (For All Ages)

- Place a generous amount of each color of paint in a small bowl. Add a small amount of glue to thicken the paint. Stir the paint and glue mixture, add more glue or paint as needed to create paint the consistency of thick finger paint.

- Look at the picture *Starry Night* with the children.

- **Say:** Vincent van Gogh was not a happy man. He suffered from depression most of his life. His one outlet was his art. Over a period of a few years, van Gogh produced more than a thousand paintings and sketches. Van Gogh loved to use thick paints to give his pictures more texture and depth. During his life people did not appreciate his art work. Today, however, van Gogh's paintings sell for millions of dollars. Look at the picture *Starry Night*. Imagine what the scene of the magi following the star would have looked like if van Gogh had painted it.

- Have the children draw simple outlines of the magi with a pencil at the bottom left corners of their sheets.

- **Say:** Van Gogh used swirly patterns for the stars and moon.

- Invite the children to draw swirling shapes in the sky above the magi. Then have the children paint around the swirling shapes with dark blue paint by using brushes or their fingers.

- Add texture by dragging a comb lightly across the top of the paint.

- Let the children use yellow and white paint to paint the pencil swirls in a twirling motion. They can use black paint to fill in the outlines of the magi. Then they can add orange accents to the swirled stars.

Adapted from PowerXpress!®Bible Experience Stations® Follow the Star © 2006 Cokesbury

Prepare

✓ Find a print or Internet image of *Starry Night* by Vincent van Gogh.

✓ Cover your work surfaces with paper or plastic.

✓ Provide: table covering; heavy paper; pencils; dark blue, yellow, white, orange, and black washable paint; paint smocks; and medium and thick brushes; glue; bowls.

Star Toss (For All Ages)

- Divide the children into groups of five children. Have the five children stand in a small circle.

- Give one child in each group a bean bag (or pair of rolled-up socks).

- Have the children gently toss the beanbag to each other in a star pattern. To make a star pattern, each child should toss the bean bag to the second person on his or her left.

- When the beanbag returns to the first child, have each child take a step backward.

- Have the children repeat the star-patterned toss.

- If one of the beanbag tosses results in the beanbag being dropped, have all of the children return to the original positions and start the game again.

Prepare

✓ Provide: one bean bag or rolled-up sock for every five children.

- Have the children continue tossing the beanbag and stepping backward to see how large a star they can make and still successfully catch the beanbag.

- **Ask:** How do you think the magi felt as they followed the star each night?

Adapted from Grow! Proclaim! Serve!: Large Group/Small Group Ages 7 & Up Leader's Guide, Winter 2014–15 © 2014 Abingdon Press

Stars Poles (For Younger Children)

- Give each child a small paper plate. Encourage the children to use glitter crayons to decorate around the edge of their paper plates.

- Give each child a star circle. Have the children glue their star circles on to the center of their paper plates.

- Let the children add star stickers all over their star circles.

- Or let the children decorate their star circles with glitter.

- Have the children put glue all over the inside of their stars.

- Place each star in a box lid or tray. Let the child sprinkle glitter over the star. Shake off the extra glitter into the box lid or tray. Reuse the extra glitter.

- Give each child a large craft stick. Tape or glue the stick to the back of the paper plate.

- Give each child several lengths of curly ribbon or crepe paper streamers. Tape or tie the ribbon or streamers to the star poles.

Star Spinners (For Older Children)

- Have the children color, cut out, and assemble the star spinners.

- **Ask:** Have you ever wondered what the star that led the magi to Bethlehem looked like?

Adapted from Grow! Proclaim! Serve!: Middle Elementary, Teacher, Winter 2013–14 © 2013 Cokesbury

Star Parade (For All Ages)

- Have the children hold their star poles or star circles and line up together.

- Play a Christmas music CD or sing "We Three Kings" as the children hold their stars and march around the room or through the church.

- End the parade in your large group area.

Prepare

✓ Photocopy and cut out the star circle (page 60) for each child.

✓ Provide: scissors, curly ribbon or crepe paper streamers, glitter crayons, glue, small paper plates, tape, large craft sticks; star stickers or glitter and box lid or tray.

Prepare

✓ Photocopy the star spinner (page 61) for each child.

✓ Provide: crayons or markers, scissors, string, tape, glue sticks, wooden dowels or extra paper.

Large Group

Bring all the children together to experience the Bible story. Ring jingle bells to alert the children to the large group time. Use the transition activity to move the children from the interest groups to the large group area.

Star Moves Relay

- Have the children line up in teams on one side of the room. Place a basket or bag with the "Star Moves" slips at the beginning of each line. Place a star picture or cut-out across from each team on the other side of the room.

- **Say:** The magi followed the star to find Jesus. Each team will move toward the star one team member at a time. The first person in the line will reach into the basket or bag and take one slip of paper. You must move across the room toward the star the way the paper tells you to move. Touch the star and then run back to the next person in line.

- Make sure everyone understands the relay and then say, "Go!"

- Continue the relay until every child has a turn.

- Encourage the children to hum "Away in a Manger" as they sit down in the large group area.

Christmas Acts

- Have the children get their star poles or star spinners and sit down in the large group area.

- Tell the story, "Magi Follow the Star" (page 56) to the children. Encourage the children to stand up and hold their star poles or twirl their star spinners each time they hear the word *star*.

- **Ask:** Why do you think God chose to announce the birth of Jesus this way? What helped the magi find their way to Jesus?

Word Play

- **Say:** The magi brought gifts to Jesus. That is how our tradition of giving gifts at Christmas began. These gifts were to honor the new king. Everyone stay seated. I'm going to play some music. While the music is playing, I will pass six gifts out to you. I want you to pass the gifts to each other the whole time the music plays. When the music stops, I want whoever is holding a gift to stand up. I want anyone who is not holding a gift to stay seated.

- Start playing lively Christmas music ("We Three Kings," "Joy to the World," "Go Tell It on the Mountain," "O Come, All Ye Faithful," and so forth).

- Pass the six gifts out to the children. Encourage them to keep passing the gifts among themselves.

Prepare

✓ Photocopy and cut apart the "Star Moves" slips (page 62) for each team. Place the slips inside a basket or bag next to the beginning of each team.

✓ Cut out a paper star or use a star picture. Tape the star on the wall across from each team within the children's reach.

Prepare

✓ Star poles and star spinners made earlier.

✓ Photocopy "Magi Follow the Star" (pages 56).

Prepare

✓ Provide: a CD with lively Christmas music, a CD player, and six empty wrapped boxes or Christmas gift bags.

✓ Write the letters in the word *CHRIST* on separate index cards. Tape a card on each box or bag.

✓ Or write a letter on each box or bag using permanent markers.

- Stop the music. Have the six children holding the gifts stand and everyone else stay seated.

- Have the children holding the six gifts come to the front.

- **Say:** Look. Each of the gifts has a letter. Please hold the gifts so everyone can see the letters.

- **Ask:** What word do you think this spells?

- Help the children arrange themselves so that the letters spell the word *Christ*.

- **Say:** Christ. The magi followed the star to find the new king, Jesus. Christ is another name for Jesus. Christ is a Christmas gift that will not break.

Word Play Review

- **Ask:** Can you remember all the Christmas gifts that we learned about? The gifts that will not break?

- Let's review.

- Use the script on pages 57–58 to review the gifts with the children.

Bible Verse Drop (For All Ages)

- Have the children spread across the play area.

- **Say:** Our Bible verse is from Matthew 2:10: When they saw the star, they were filled with joy.

- Have the children repeat the verse after you.

- **Ask:** I wonder what the magi did to show their joy? What do you do to show joy?

- Encourage the children to show joy. They might shout, dance, jump, clap, and so forth.

- Have the children be still.

- Show the children the paper star.

- **Say:** Watch me. I'm going to say the Bible verse again and hold up the star. Then I'm going to drop the star and let it flutter to the ground. While the star is dropping, I want you to show as much joy as you can.

- Make sure the children understand the game. Hold up the star and say the Bible verse. Then drop the star. Have the children move and make noise and then cut them off when the star hits the ground.

- Play the game several times, saying the Bible verse each time. Vary the time between the end of the Bible verse and when you drop the star to build anticipation.

Prepare
✓ Photocopy Word Play Review (pages 57–58).

Prepare
✓ Provide: paper star cut-out.

Small Groups

Divide the children into small groups. You may organize the groups around age-levels or around readers and nonreaders. Keep the groups small, with a maximum of ten children in each group. You may need to have more than one of each group.

Young Children

- Show the children the Advent wreath.

- **Say:** We light the first candle on the Advent wreath to help us remember hope.

- Light the first Advent candle.

- **Say:** We light the second candle on the Advent wreath to help us remember love.

- Light the second Advent candle.

- **Say:** We light the third candle on the Advent wreath to help us remember joy.

- Light the third Advent candle.

- **Say:** We light the fourth candle on the Advent wreath to help us remember peace. When Jesus was born, a multitude of angels sang praise to God and promised peace on earth.

- Light the fourth Advent candle.

- **Say:** We light the Christ candle to remember Jesus, God's gift to the whole world.

- Light the Christ candle. Let the candles burn for a few minutes and then blow them out.

- **Say:** The magi followed the star to find Jesus, the Christ. They honored Jesus with their gifts.

- **Ask:** What gifts can you give to Jesus?

- **Say:** Christ is a gift that won't break. You have been helping others with the baby items you have brought to share with families that do not have the things they need for their new babies. Along with these items, we are giving these families the unbreakable gifts of hope, love, joy, and peace.

- Look at some of the new baby items the children brought. Let the children decide if Mary and Joseph would have had such an item or something similar to it.

- Celebrate with a party. Enjoy the painted star cookies. Look at the ideas on pages 4–5 for games and other snacks.

- Close with a prayer.

Prepare

✓ Set up an Advent wreath with four purple candles and one white candle.

✓ Provide: matches. (For adult use only. Keep the matches out of the children's reach.)

✓ Look at pages 4–5 for party ideas.

✓ Make plans to deliver the new baby items to a homeless shelter, battered women's shelter, or food pantry.

Christmas Gifts That Won't Break: Children's Leader Guide

Older Children

- Show the children the Advent wreath.

- **Say:** We light the first candle on the Advent wreath to help us remember hope.

- Light the first Advent candle.

- **Say:** We light the second candle on the Advent wreath to help us remember love.

- Light the second Advent candle.

- **Say:** We light the third candle on the Advent wreath to help us remember joy.

- Light the third Advent candle.

- **Say:** We light the fourth candle on the Advent wreath to help us remember peace. When Jesus was born, a multitude of angels sang praise to God and promised peace on earth.

- Light the fourth Advent candle.

- **Say:** We light the Christ candle to remember Jesus, God's gift to the whole world.

- Light the Christ candle. Let the candles burn for a few minutes and then blow them out.

- **Say:** The magi followed the star to find Jesus, the Christ. They honored Jesus with their gifts.

- **Ask:** What gifts can you give to Jesus?

- **Say:** Christ is a gift that won't break. You have been helping others with the baby items you have brought to share with families that do not have the things they need for their new babies. Along with these items, we are giving these families the unbreakable gifts of hope, love, joy, and peace.

- Look at some of the new baby items the children brought. Let the children decide if Mary and Joseph would have had such an item or something similar to it.

- Celebrate with a party. Enjoy the painted star cookies. Look at the ideas on pages 4–5 for games and other snacks.

- Close with a prayer.

Prepare

✓ Set up an Advent wreath with four purple candles and one white candle.

✓ Provide: matches. (For adult use only. Keep the matches out of the children's reach.)

✓ Look at pages 4–5 for party ideas.

✓ Make plans to deliver the new baby items to a homeless shelter, battered women's shelter, or food pantry.

Magi Follow the Star

by Beth Parr and Daphna Flegal

(Have the children stand up and hold their star poles or twirl their star spinners each time they hear the word star.)

When baby Jesus was born there were some magi who lived far away in another country. These men liked to study the **stars**.

One night the magi noticed a strange new **star** shining in the sky.

The magi believed that this new **star** was a sign, telling them that a new king had been born.

The magi decided to follow the **star** and find the new king.

The magi packed for a long journey. They packed clothes and food. They packed special gifts to give to the new king.

The magi traveled at night, following the light of the **star**. They traveled for months and months.

The **star** led the magi to the city of Jerusalem. When they arrived in the city the went to the see King Herod.

"Where is the new king?" asked the magi. "We have been following his **star**. We want to worship him."

When King Herod heard this, he was not happy. He was afraid that he might not get to keep being king.

King Herod called together his smartest helpers. He asked, "Where will the new king be born?"

The helpers thought and thought. Then they remembered that the prophets had written that a special leader for the people would be born in Bethlehem. The helpers told King Herod what the prophets said.

Herod called the magi to come and see him again. "Go to Bethlehem," said King Herod. "Find this child. Come back and tell me where he is, so I can worship him, too."

The magi continued on their journey. They were excited when they saw the big beautiful **star** in the sky once more. The magi followed the **star**. The **star** stopped over a house in Bethlehem.

The magi quickly climbed down from their camels and went into the house.

When they stepped into the house, the magi saw Mary and Joseph and Jesus. Jesus was the new king!

The magi got down on their knees and worshiped Jesus.

The magi had special gifts for Jesus. One magi gave Jesus a gift of gold.

Another magi gave Jesus a gift of frankincense. Frankincense has a very sweet smell. The people used it when they worshiped God.

The other magi gave Jesus a gift of myrrh. Myrrh also had a strong smell. It was used to make perfumes and lotions.

The magi gave Jesus gifts because they wanted to honor Jesus. Jesus was the new king who God sent to help people know more about God.

After the magi left Jesus, they had a dream. In the dream they were warned not to see King Herod again.

So the magi climbed back on their camels and went home by a different way. They did not tell King Herod about Jesus.

Let's say our Bible verse together:

When they saw the **star**, they were filled with joy.

–Matthew 2:10

Christmas Gifts That Won't Break: Children's Leader Guide

Word Play Review

Leader: Welcome to today's Trivia Game, Word Play Review! Let's divide the audience into two teams.

(Divide the children into two teams. Have the children stay seated in their teams.)

Leader: I need two volunteers to begin the game.

(Choose one child from each team to come to the front of the room and stand on either side of the leader.)

Leader: Fantastic! Now, here's how we'll play the game. I'll read a question. Whoever makes the buzzer sound will be the first person to answer the question. Teammates, you can help by shouting out the answers. Before we begin, contestants I want you to practice making the buzzer sound.

(Have the two children make a buzzer sound.)

Leader: Great! Teams are you ready? Let's begin. **Question 1:** True or False? Joseph was an electrician.

(Have the children make the buzzer sound and answer the question.)

Leader: The answer is false! Joseph was a carpenter. Thank you, contestants. Now, I need two more volunteers.

(Choose a child from each team to be new contestants.)

Leader: Question 2: Who came to Joseph in a dream?

(Have the children make the buzzer sound and answer the question.)

Leader: The answer is an angel. Thank you, contestants. Now, I need two more volunteers.

(Choose a child from each team to be new contestants.)

Leader: Question 3: The first candle on the Advent wreath and the first Christmas gift that won't break is the gift of what?

(Have the children make the buzzer sound and answer the question.)

Leader: The answer is hope. Hope is a Christmas gift that won't break. Thank you, contestants. Now, I need two more volunteers.

(Choose a child from each team to be new contestants.)

Leader: Question 4: True or False: Jesus was born in Bethlehem.

(Have the children make the buzzer sound and answer the question.)

Leader: The answer is true! Jesus was born in Bethlehem. Thank you, contestants. Now, I need two more volunteers.

(Choose a child from each team to be new contestants.)

Leader: Question 5: What was the name of Jesus' mother?

(Have the children make the buzzer sound and answer the question.)

Leader: That's right, Jesus' mother was Mary. Thank you, contestants. Now, let's have two more volunteers.

(Choose a child from each team to be new contestants.)

Leader: Question 6: The second candle on the Advent wreath and the second Christmas gift that won't break is the gift of what?

(Have the children make the buzzer sound and answer the question.)

Leader: The answer is love. Love is a Christmas gift that won't break. Thank you, contestants. Now, I need two more volunteers.

(Choose a child from each team to be new contestants.)

Leader: Question 7: True or False: An angel told the bricklayers the good news about baby Jesus.

(Have the children make the buzzer sound and answer the question.)

Leader: The answer is false! Who did the angels tell the good news about Jesus? *(pause)* That's right, the shepherds. Thank you, contestants. Now, I need two more volunteers.

(Choose a child from each team to be new contestants.)

Leader: Question 8: The third candle on the Advent wreath and the third Christmas gift that won't break is the gift of what?

(Have the children make the buzzer sound and answer the question.)

Leader: The answer is joy. Joy is a Christmas gift that won't break. Thank you, contestants. Now, I need two more volunteers.

(Choose a child from each team to be new contestants.)

Leader: Question 9: After the angel's message, how many angels appeared to the shepherds?

(Have the children make the buzzer sound and answer the question.)

Leader: The answer is a multitude, or a whole bunch! Now, I need two more volunteers.

(Choose a child from each team to be new contestants.)

Leader: Question 10: True or False: The angels sang about peace on earth.

(Have the children make the buzzer sound and answer the question.)

Leader: The answer is a true. Thank you, contestants. Now, I need two more volunteers.

(Choose a child from each team to be new contestants.)

Leader: Question 11: The fourth candle on the Advent wreath and the fourth Christmas gift that won't break is the gift of what?

(Have the children make the buzzer sound and answer the question.)

Leader: The answer is peace. Peace is a Christmas gift that won't break. Thank you, contestants. Now, I need two more volunteers.

(Choose a child from each team to be new contestants.)

Leader: Question 12: What appeared in the sky to mark the birth of a new king?

(Have the children make the buzzer sound and answer the question.)

Leader: a star! The star led the magi to the new king. Thank you, contestants. Now, I need two more volunteers.

(Choose a child from each team to be new contestants.)

Leader: That leads us to our last question. What is the candle we light on Christmas Day, and what is the fifth Christmas gift that won't break?

Leader: Christ! Christ is a Christmas gift that won't break. Thank you, contestants. And thank you, teams, for playing WORD PLAY REVIEW!

Christmas Gifts That Won't Break: Children's Leader Guide

Star Pictures

Lesson 5: The Gift of Christ

Star Circle

Christmas Gifts That Won't Break: Children's Leader Guide

Star Spinners/Parade

1. Color the Star Parade Spinner.
2. Cut out the spinner along the dark lines.
3. Cut towards the center of the spinner along the four thick dark lines.
4. Fold the flaps upwards along the dashed lines as shown below.
5. Roll the Star Spinner into a cone shape.
6. Make a knot in the end of a piece of string and tape it inside the cone as shown. The string should extend out of the cone through the point.
7. Glue the side tab to the back of the other edge.
8. Attach the end of the string to a wooden dowel or a folded piece of paper.
9. Hold the stick and wave it back and forth. Watch the stars go around.

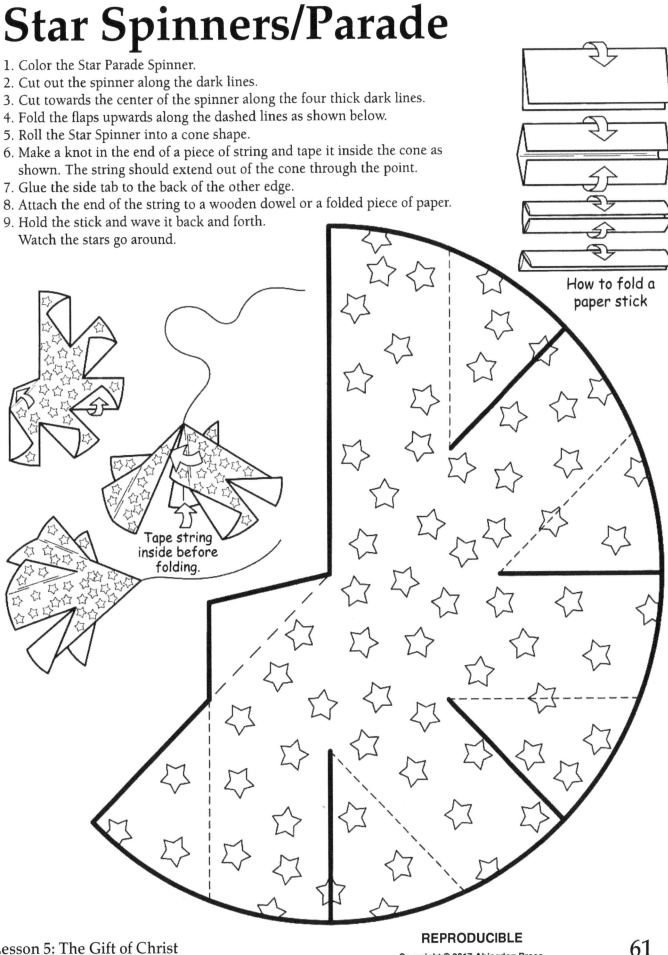

How to fold a paper stick

Tape string inside before folding.

Lesson 5: The Gift of Christ

Star Moves

Walk like a camel.

Walk like a donkey.

Crawl like a baby.

Tiptoe quietly.

Walk backward.

Pretend to rock a baby as you walk.

Jump for joy as you move forward.

Look up and point at the sky as you walk.

Sing "We Three Kings" as you walk.

Stop every three steps and say, "Look, a star!"

Suggestions for an All-Church Event

Christmas Gifts That Won't Break encourages people to experience God's gifts of hope, love, joy, and peace during the Advent season. These gifts never break! Author James W. Moore reminds us that material things wear out, break, erode, go out of fashion, and can be lost or stolen. He invites us to build our happiness on things we cannot lose.

A churchwide Advent program for all ages will help people learn more about the unbreakable gifts God offers through the birth of Jesus, gifts that give us more abundant life. It will offer opportunities for learning, for intergenerational projects and activities, and for reaching out to the community with hope, joy, love, and peace. The following resources are available:

Christmas Gifts That Won't Break:
Expanded Edition with Devotions
by James W. Moore with Jacob Armstrong

James W. Moore
Christmas Gifts That Won't Break:
A Youth Study

James W. Moore
Christmas Gifts That Won't Break:
A Children's Leader Guide

Also available for adult small group study:

James W. Moore with Jacob Armstrong
Christmas Gifts That Won't Break:
Leader Guide

James W. Moore with Jacob Armstrong
Christmas Gifts That Won't Break:
DVD

Schedule

Many churches have weeknight programs that include an evening meal, an intergenerational gathering time, and classes for children, youth, and adults. The following schedule illustrates one way to organize a weeknight program.

5:30	Meal
6:00	Intergenerational gathering introducing Advent gifts and the lighting of the Advent candles. The time may include presentations, skits, music, and opening or closing prayers.
6:15–8:45	Classes for Children, Youth, and Adults

Churches may want to do the Advent study as a Sunday school program. This setting would be similar to the weeknight setting. The following schedule takes into account a shorter class time, which is the norm for Sunday morning programs.

10 minutes	Intergenerational Gathering
45 minutes	Classes for Children, Youth, and Adults

Choose a schedule that works best for your congregation and its existing Christian education programs.

Activity Suggestions

All-Church Missions Baby Shower

Ask participants to bring new baby items to give to a homeless shelter, battered women's shelter, or food pantry. End the mission project with a party. Snacks and games can be found in the children's study.

Family Advent Wreaths

Directions for making simple Advent wreaths can be found in Lesson 1 of the children's study.

Advent Candle Lighting

You may choose to use the following prayers (also found in the adult study guide) as part of lighting the Advent candles during worship:

First Sunday of Advent: The Gift of Hope

Leader: "The unbreakable gift for this first Sunday of Advent is the gift of hope."

Light the first candle.

Pray: Dear God, thank you for the season of Advent and the gift of hope. Help us to prepare our hearts for your coming and to remember the true meaning of Christmas. Amen.

Second Sunday of Advent: The Gift of Love

Leader: "The unbreakable gift for this second Sunday of Advent is the gift of love."

Light two candles.

Pray: Dear God, thank you for the gift of love. May we share this gift with others and learn how to love unconditionally. Help us during this Christmas season to practice love in action with family, friends, and strangers. Amen.

Third Sunday of Advent: The Gift of Joy

Leader: "The unbreakable gift for this third Sunday of Advent is the gift of joy."

Light three candles.

Pray: Dear God, thank you for the gift of joy and for the way it brightens our days. Help us to give joy to others through what we say and do. Show us how to make this Christmas a true season of joy. Amen.

Fourth Sunday of Advent: The Gift of Peace

Leader: "The unbreakable gift for this fourth Sunday of Advent is the gift of peace."

Light four candles.

Pray: Dear God, thank you for the gift of peace. Help us to put peace into practice in our lives and to show others the path to true peace. Remind us to serve as peacemakers and to share the love of God with those in need. Amen.

Christmas Day: The Gift of Christ

Leader: "The unbreakable gift for Christmas day is the gift of Christ."

Light the Christ candle.

Pray: Dear God, thank you for the gift of Christ. Help us to put hope, love, joy, and peace into practice in our lives and to show others how being followers of Christ Jesus changes our hearts and lives. Amen.

Bible Verses for Lesson 3

see pages 32-33

I will celebrate and rejoice in you;

I will sing praises to your name, Most High.

(Psalm 9:2)

Clap your hands, all you people!

Shout joyfully to God with a joyous shout!

(Psalm 47:1)

Our mouths were suddenly filled with laughter;

our tongues were filled with joyful shouts.

It was even said, at that time, among the nations,

"The LORD has done great things for them!"

(Psalm 126:2)

The angel said, "Don't be afraid! Look!

I bring good news to you—wonderful, joyous news for all people."

(Luke 2:10)

When they saw the star, they were filled with joy.

(Matthew 2:10)

"I have said these things to you so that my joy will be in you

and your joy will be complete."

(John 15:11)

Bonus Coloring Page

CPSIA information can be obtained
at www.ICGtesting.com
Printed in the USA
BVHW010213051121
620863BV00013B/458